One
Church,
Four
Generations

One Church, Four Generations

Understanding and Reaching All Ages in Your Church

Gary L. McIntosh

Baker Books

A Division of Baker Book House Co
Grand Rapids, Michigan 49516

© 2002 by Gary L. McIntosh

Published by Baker Books
a division of Baker Publishing Group
P.O. Box 6287, Grand Rapids, MI 49516-6287
www.bakerbooks.com

Seventh printing, September 2008

Printed in the United States of America

Library of Congress Cataloging-in-Publication Data
McIntosh, Gary, 1947–
    One church, four generations : understanding and reaching all ages in your church / Gary L. McIntosh.
        p.   cm.
    Includes bibliographical references (p.   ).
    ISBN 10: 0-8010-9137-3
    ISBN 978-0-8010-9137-7
    1. Intergenerational relations—Religious aspects—Christianity. 2. Church. I. McIntosh, Gary, 1947- Three generations. II. Title.
BV640 .M22 2002
261.8´342—dc21   2002001512

Parts of this book were previously published by Revell with the title *Three Generations* © 1995 by Gary L. McIntosh.

Unless otherwise indicated, Scripture is taken from the New American Standard Bible®, Copyright © 1960, 1962, 1963, 1968, 1971, 1972, 1973, 1975, 1977, 1995 by The Lockman Foundation. Used by permission.

Scripture marked NLT is taken from the *Holy Bible*, New Living Translation, copyright © 1996. Used by permission of Tyndale House Publishers, Inc., Wheaton, Illinois 60189. All rights reserved.

Dedicated to the Builders in my life:

My grandmother, Wilma Thompson, who faithfully read the Bible in my presence as I was growing up and gave me my first knowledge of God and his church.

My mother, Billie C. McIntosh, who sacrificially gave me everything she never had as a child growing up in the Great Depression and constantly encouraged me in my education and ministry.

My father- and mother-in-law, Bill and Amelia Kurylow, who loved me as their own son and entrusted me with their daughter.

Nelle Roberts and David and Gladys Bishop, faithful servants of our Lord who introduced me to Jesus Christ as my Lord and Savior.

Rev. Erwin and Mrs. Wilna Ericson, who taught me the Word of God and gave me my first opportunities to serve Christ.

Rev. Bob and Mrs. Louise Duggan, who put up with my youthful exuberance and helped polish my rough edges.

Rev. Dennis and Mrs. Shirley Perkins, colaborers in the faith who befriended me as a young seminary student and helped me gain confidence as a pastor.

Lord, Thou hast been our dwelling place
in all generations.

Psalm 90:1

Contents

Preface

There was a time not long ago when church leaders tried to minister to people as a single mass. No longer. Today's church leaders understand that ministry must take place among a mosaic of groups and subgroups—most notably generational cohorts.

Interest in generational research and studies has grown stronger as the world rushed into the twenty-first century. A good example of this interest was recently observed with the opening of the Ellis Island web site on April 17, 2001. A seven-year, 22.5-million-dollar project transcribing ship passenger manifests for the Port of New York between 1892 and 1924 was finished and placed on the web (www.ellisislandrecords.org). Officials expected heavy traffic but not the large number who logged on immediately. More than eighty thousand people logged onto the site at its opening and an estimated half million others were turned away! Traffic has dropped off some since then but remains steady at about forty to sixty thousand visitors a day.

The reason for the massive interest in the Ellis Island Foundation project relates directly to people's interest in generations. It is estimated that nearly 40 percent of Americans can trace a relative back to Ellis Island. Genealogists indicate that about six in ten Americans are researching their family history in an effort to shed light on the past—and future! What drives the desire to study generations? A large part of it is the search for greater understanding of ourselves.

Historically, four generations often exist together, interlaced in a particular moment of time: young, adult, mature, and senior. Today these four generations are called the Bridgers, Busters, Boomers, and Builders.

Not only are there four generations existing together, but there are four sets of value systems that are being advanced, each with its perceived needs and perspectives. When church leaders understand each generation's values, and how they were molded by events that define the generation, they can be more faithful in their use of limited resources to effectively fulfill the Great Commission.

The focus in the original edition of this book—*Three Generations*—was on the three older generations. At that time the Bridger generation was too young for many accurate predictions of their characteristics to be made. However, over the last seven years, Bridgers have gone through enough common experiences that a generational mystique is developing, a generational identity that touches all within their cohort in some way. While insights regarding the Bridger generation must be held loosely, due to the fact that they are still developing, there is enough information to begin building a helpful picture.

This new edition of the book builds on the first by adding information from new research on this newest generation to move into the spotlight. Also a few corrections of the first edition have been made, along with an updating of numerous facts and statistics.

It is my prayer that this new edition will continue to serve as a helpful resource as we together seek to win many precious souls from all generations to our Lord and Savior Jesus Christ. As the writer of Psalm 89 exclaims:

> I will sing of the lovingkindness of the LORD forever; To all generations I will make known Thy faithfulness with my mouth.
>
> Psalm 89:1

Waves
of Change

S cripture uses the word *generation* in three different ways. It can be an age group in a family, a period of time, or a group of people connected by their place in time. The genealogical tables found in Genesis and Matthew are obvious examples of the first. When the Psalmist writes, "I will cause Thy name to be remembered in all generations" (Ps. 45:17), he could have said "in all times" or "in all ages," which is an example of the second. However, the third definition is what I am thinking of in *One Church, Four Generations*. A generation is a group of people who are connected by their place in time with common boundaries and a common character.

The study of generational change has been an important aspect of my life since 1983. In July of that year I left a seven-year pastorate to become vice president of consulting services for Dr. Win Arn at the Institute for American Church Growth, then located in Pasadena, California.

Shortly after I arrived, one of my fellow consultants, Rev. Robert Orr, shared some thoughts he had on the Baby Boom generation and their impact on churches. The interest he created was intensified about one year later while I was traveling by plane to a consulting assignment in New Jersey.

While on the plane, I found a November 5, 1984, copy of *U.S. News and World Report* and began reading its major article "Here

Come the Baby Boomers." When I finished reading that article, I was hooked. For the past eighteen years, I've read, clipped, and filed just about every article I could find on generational issues. I honestly do not know how many articles I have collected, but the file that contains them is more than three feet thick.

In 1986 I became professor of Christian Ministry and Leadership at Talbot School of Theology (Biola University), where I teach courses on church growth, evangelism, and leadership. The study of generational change has continued to be one of my prime interests, and being a professor has given me the opportunity to pursue it. During the past eighteen years, I have spoken on generational change at denominational conferences, local churches, and seminars. I have also written several articles on the topic.

Why Another Book on Generations?

There were very few books on the topic of Baby Boomers in 1983 and none on Baby Busters or the Bridgers. Today as I review the books available, I can easily name more than fifty dealing with one or more of the generations. In the collection of books I have on generations, many are on the Boomers. Some are secular books, such as Paul C. Light's groundbreaking *Baby Boomers*. Others focus on the challenge Boomers bring to the church, such as Doug Murren's *The Baby Boomerang*. Still others, like Cheryl Russell's *100 Predictions for the Baby Boom,* offer insights on the future of the Boomer generation.

Among the first books to address the uniqueness of the Buster generation were William Dunn's *The Baby Bust: A Generation Comes of Age* and Steven Gibb's *Twentysomething, Floundering, and Off the Yuppie Track*. Since those books hit the shelves, a large number of books have expounded on the characteristics and future of the Baby Bust. Among the newer books focusing on Baby Busters are *The Invisible Generation* by George Barna, *Inside the Soul of a New Generation* by Tim Celek and Dieter Zander, and *Generating Hope* by Jimmy Long. Two helpful books were written by Busters Todd Hahn and David Verhaagen, *Reckless Hope: Understanding and Reaching Baby Busters and GenXers after God.*

As might be expected, few books have focused on the Bridger generation. This youngest generation is just coming of age, and more books discussing their attributes will be coming in the future. However, the first book to attempt an analysis of Bridgers is *The Bridger Generation* by Dr. Thom Rainer.

Generational change has become quite a popular topic, and the book that seemed to start it all was Ken Dychtwald's *Age Wave.* This book alerted people to the aging of America. Then William Strauss and Neil Howe released their massive study, *Generations: The History of America's Future 1584 to 2069.* It has been reviewed and quoted in numerous publications and will likely form the foundation for future studies on the issue. Additional books on generational themes continue to find an audience. *Rocking the Ages* by J. Walker Smith and Ann Clurman reported on marketing to the various generations. The most popular book to expound a generational theme is *The Greatest Generation* by Tom Brokaw. First published in 1998, its popularity produced spin-offs of audiotapes and CD versions, as well as several tagalong books offering personal insights from the Builder generation.

My interest in generational issues, however, goes much deeper than a mere intellectual study. I have often felt a special kinship with Timothy, who was raised by his grandmother, Lois, and his mother, Eunice (2 Tim. 1:5). I too was raised by my grandmother and my mother. Ours was a multigenerational home—my grandmother was born in 1896, my mother was born in 1923, and I'm an older Boomer. Generational issues were always a topic of discussion in our home. Today I am the father of two Baby Buster children and three Bridger grandchildren. I continue to have a concern that generations work together.

As I have traveled, consulting with churches and leading church growth seminars during the past eighteen years, I have noticed that most churches target one generation exclusively—Builders or Boomers or Busters or Bridgers—while often ignoring the others. Most books and articles on the topic also seem to target a single generation.

As pastors and church leaders, most of us do not have the choice of working with only one generation. In most of our churches all generations are present, and we must build a ministry that includes them all.

That is why I have written *One Church, Four Generations*. While I certainly do not have all of the answers, I believe this book will assist pastors, church leaders, and laypersons to keep all four generations in view and gain some insights into ways to integrate the generations for effective ministry.

Readers of the first edition have found this book helped them to understand the challenges of synthesizing all generations under one ministry. Many describe how they gained a better perspective on each generation, as well as practical strategies for effective ministry to each one. Gaining insight into the undercurrents and discontent that exist between generations has been for many well worth the price of the book. Almost all described the first edition as a must read for doing ministry well in our day.

The Panoramic Approach

As I contemplated writing this book, I was faced with two possible approaches. I could write the book with a microscopic view, attempting to cover every detail, aspect, and nuance of each generation. Or I could write the book with more of a panoramic view, presenting the larger picture with a few aspects of each generation standing out like trees in a landscape.

I have chosen to take the panoramic approach, and thus broad generalizations about each generation should be expected. There are aspects of each generation that may not be highlighted as much as some may wish. I have not delved into the differences that minorities and various ethnic or immigrant groups might encounter. Nor have I touched on the differences created by geography, education, or economic conditions. In most cases, however, the generalizations suggested will fit about three-fourths of the members of the generation.

It is my hope that you will be able to identify enough with the insights suggested that you will gain a better understanding of the issues involved in ministering to multiple generational groups in your church. Working together in love is a key aspect of a healthy church (John 13:34–35).

Four Generational Waves

If you had to put everyone in the United States into four groups, how would you do it? On what basis would you group them? Would you use geographic location, educational background, income level, or entertainment preferences as determining factors? It would depend on your purpose.

If you had to put everyone in your church into four groups, how would you divide them? Since your purpose is ministry, finding common denominators for the people in your congregation could help you minister to them more effectively.

Certain people in your congregation are connected by a place in time, by common boundaries, and by a common character. We can say that those people are of one generation. Their ages may vary widely, but they tend to identify with each other because of national or world events they have all experienced, fads they have enjoyed, or prominent people they have come to know. They tend to share certain character traits or characteristics that reflect their time in history. The group is loosely held together by these experiential threads and by some common beliefs. They do some things in ways unique to the group, and they tend to see differences between themselves and members of other groups.

As we study American society today, we see that there are groups of people with shared characteristics and similar interests. We can fit most people into four broad groups.

Those who range in age from the late fifties and up can be called the Builders; the Boomers are those in their late thirties to mid fifties; young adults in their twenties to late thirties are the Busters, and those younger than twenty are the Bridgers.

As a generation moves through time, it causes a generational wave. Many members of a group will move through childhood, young adulthood, midlife, and retirement as a group, although the youngest and oldest members of the group will experience these phases at different times. As the group moves along, it creates changes or waves that are identified specifically with that generation. The larger the generation, the larger the wave it creates.

Ever since the beginning of the twentieth century, Americans have been fond of placing labels on groups of people that influence our culture. Remember these? bobby-soxers (1940s), beatniks (1950s), hippies (1960s), preppies (1970s), Valley Girls (1980s), and Gen Xers (1990s).

The influence of most of these groups was fairly small. They created little more than a stirring up of the sand on the beaches of change. However, when the Boomer wave between 1946 and 1964 crashed against the shores of change, we all took notice.

The Boomer wave is a generation bounded by the end of World War II and the decline of the high birth rate beginning in 1965. (Nineteen sixty-four was the last year with a birth rate of more than four million until 1989 when births once again reached that mark.) These boundaries set this generation apart from past generations and those that would follow. Like a tidal wave, we measure all other waves against it, particularly the waves just before and after it—the Builder wave and the Buster wave.[1]

The Builder Wave

The Builder wave came just before the Boomers. A get-it-done generation, Builders comprise two main groups, called the G.I. generation and the Silent generation. Influential members of this group include Bob Hope, John Kennedy, Ronald Reagan, and Billy Graham. Builders tend to be loyal, faithful, and committed. Today most are in their sixties or older and remember the Depression, World War II, and days with no TV.

The Boomer Wave

The Boomer Generation is the largest and most studied generation in U.S. history. It comprises two major groups: the Leading-Edge Boomers (LEBs) and the Trailing-Edge Boomers

(TREBs). Influential members of this generation include Spike Lee, Oprah Winfrey, Sylvester Stallone, Connie Chung, and George W. Bush. Boomers have earned a reputation for being rebellious, affluent, and independent. Most are in their forties and fifties. They have lived during a strong economy, they vividly remember the war in Vietnam, and they cannot imagine the world without TV.

The Buster Wave

The generation that follows the Boomers is the Busters, born between 1965 and 1983. They are called Busters because their generation is smaller than the Boomer generation. They divide into two main subgroups: the Bust and the Boomlet. Influential members include Johnny Depp, Winona Ryder, Whitney Houston, and Greg Maddux. Now in their twenties and thirties, Busters may be the most abused, forgotten, and alienated generation of the four. This current generation of young adults has experienced a fluctuating economy, Desert Storm, and MTV.

The Bridger Wave

The newest generation is the Bridgers. They are just coming to an age where their characteristics are identifiable, and early evidence indicates they are technologically astute, tolerant of diversity, and superfragmented regarding their preferences. All of them are below twenty years old, are experiencing a volatile economy and the war on terror against Afghanistan's Taliban rulers, and live in the highly interactive world of the Internet, cell phones, and personal digital assistants.

Changing Generational Waves

Anyone observing our culture today can easily see that drastic changes have been taking place, signaling that the influence of the senior generation is waning and that of the younger generations is growing.

The Political Signal

Beginning with the 1988 presidential campaign, Americans have focused on generational changes. George Bush described the coming generational change as a relay runner getting prepared to hand off the baton to the next generation. The *New York Times* highlighted this changing generational scene with its major headline for Wednesday, August 17, 1988: "Bush Chooses Senator Quayle of Indiana, a 41-year-old Conservative, for No. 2 Spot." Subheadings to that lead article included "Emphasis on Youth" and "Baby Boomer with Right Credentials." Quayle, who was born February 4, 1947, became the first Baby Boomer to be on a national ticket. This was a highly visible signal that the torch was being passed to another generation, and it marked the start of a journey into the future.

If the choice of Dan Quayle as George Bush's running mate in 1988 indicated the handing off of the baton, then the election of Bill Clinton and Al Gore in 1992 clearly pushed the Boomer generation to the finish line. Noting the generational change taking place during the 1992 presidential election, newspaper headlines read, "Nation Poised to Elect New Generation" and "Time of Leadership Comes to 'Baby Boomers.'"

Bill Nichols, writing in *USA Today*'s weekend edition of July 10–12, 1992, noted, ". . . in Clinton's selection Thursday of the Tennessee senator as his running mate, a torch has been passed. For the first time, a presidential ticket has two candidates born after World War II—children of Vietnam instead of Vichy, the Temptations rather than Tommy Dorsey, and *All in the Family* not *Ozzie and Harriet*."[2] Quoted in the same article, Gore said, "Throughout American history each generation has passed on leadership to the next. That time has come again."

An interesting observation regarding the comparative ages of presidential candidates is that, until the 1990s, the older of two presidential candidates was usually the winner. In fact in the thirty-five elections leading up to 1996, the older candidate was victorious twenty-three times, or two-thirds of the elections. As examples, consider the following. In 1856 Buchanan was 65 and Fremont 43. Buchanan won. In 1864 Lincoln was 55 and McClellan 38. Lincoln won. In 1948 Truman was 64 and Dewey 46. Truman won. In 1984 Reagan was 73 and Mondale 56. Reagan won. Then in 1992, when Bush was 68 and Clinton 46, Clinton won. When Bill Clinton moved into the White House, he was twenty-two years younger than his predecessor, George Bush. Only John F. Kennedy entered the presidency with a larger generation gap. He was twenty-seven years younger than outgoing President Dwight D. Eisenhower. Again in the 1996 election, Dole was 73 and Clinton 50. Clinton won. However, the 2000 presidential election returned to the predictable pattern as fifty-four-year-old George W. Bush defeated fifty-two-year-old Al Gore, Jr.

The TV Signal

Perhaps more than anywhere else, generational change in our society is evident in the television we watch. Changes occurring in network broadcasting mirror the changes in our society, as producers attempt to reach the largest possible audience. The majority of programs are geared to the eighteen- to thirty-four year olds—the older Bridgers and most Busters. During the years when many Boomers were reaching their thirties, television programs began to include more sex, offensive language, and controversial societal issues than ever allowed before. By the time the Busters came along, television series had themes that were cynical and ironically detached. This was also true in films, such as *Slacker,* and television shows, like *Reality Bites.* Today's television programming presents a new earnestness that often addresses issues such as substance abuse, by providing two sides to the story and letting viewers make their own choice. Most popular are *Dawson's Creek, Felicity,* and *7th Heaven.*

In 1990 forty-one-year-old Jay Leno took over the *Tonight Show* from Johnny Carson, who was retiring at age sixty-five after thirty years as the show's host. The selection of Leno was an attempt to hold on to a portion of Carson's Builder audience but it was also designed to attract the Boomers and Busters.

Later, Star Trek fans saw the theme of generational change reflected in the TV series *Star Trek: The Next Generation.* It was sort of a passing of the generational baton from Captain Kirk to Captain Picard. The *Star Trek* series continued to undergo development with *Star Trek: Deep Space Nine* and *Star Trek: Voyager* in an attempt to keep up with the changing generations of viewers.

The Religious Signal

Depending on whose research study you read, the typical church in the United States still has an average of only seventy-five to one hundred people attending worship each Sunday morning.[3] Yet approximately every three weeks another church enters the league of a "megachurch."

To be a megachurch, a church must have a minimum of two thousand members. In 1970 there were only ten such churches. Today it is estimated that more than eight thousand megachurches exist in the United States.[4]

In part, the megachurch boom is due to the Baby Boom. Older Boomers who shied away from church for years returned to religion in fairly large numbers during the late 1980s and early 1990s. The fortysomething Boomers were searching for personal meaning, religious education for their children, and answers to age-old questions.

This midlife generation (as well as their Buster children and Bridger grandchildren) often looks for a less traditional and ritualistic church with a contemporary message, music, and ministry. The decline of denominations, the growth of private Christian schools, the birth of specialized ministries such as MOPS (Mothers of Preschoolers), and the debut of celebrative worship services featuring contemporary music and drama are all signals of generational change.

Similar to the political shift described before, a wave of generational change is taking place among church, denominational, and parachurch leadership. Pastor Greg Laurie of the Harvest Christian Fellowship of Riverside, California, is an example. Thirty years ago nineteen-year-old Laurie started a Bible study with thirty people. Today forty-nine-year-old Laurie's Harvest Church is one of the largest churches in the United States.

Laurie has become one of our nation's new religious leaders through his annual Harvest Crusade. Since 1990 more than one million people have attended this contemporary version of a Billy Graham crusade. In place of a large mass choir singing "Just as I Am," the audience at a Harvest Crusade hears Christian bluegrass, pop, and rock songs belted out by a band that includes singers, a drummer, and guitarists.

The 2001 crusade featured Christian rock concerts, skateboard exhibitions, and car shows.

Harvest Christian Fellowship also embraces cyberchurch growth. The church is at the forefront of churches seeking viable uses for the Internet. Each week live cybercasts of Sunday services are available, along with archives of past sermons and an on-line store featuring church apparel, books, and tapes. The site is supported by the E-team, a group of volunteers who, through the web site, spread the word about Christ and the church. During the recent crusade fifty volunteers transmitted the event to www.harvest.org.

Serving the Generations

Clearly there is a new generational wave hitting the shore in the United States. No doubt additional illustrations of this fact could be added, but the three signals given—politics, television, and religion—picture the changes quite nicely.

Why, though, should these changes concern us in the church? Our God is a changeless God as evident in Scriptures: "For I, the LORD, do not change" (Mal. 3:6) and "Jesus Christ is the same yesterday and today, yes and forever" (Heb. 13:8). Yet, while we affirm that God is changeless and his truth unchangeable, we also recognize that generations change and Scripture records that it normally takes new leadership to communicate to new generations. Perhaps the best example in the Bible is that of Moses and Joshua. God selected Moses to lead the children of Israel out of the land of Egypt, but he used Joshua, not Moses, to reach a new generation in a new land.

Failure to understand and respond to the changing generational influences in the United States may have negative impact on our churches and ministry. Here are five of the several possible results.

1. *A slow decline for many local churches and related denominations.* The membership of churches that are able to understand the changing generational dynamics appears to be growing, while those that cannot understand and adjust to the changing generations are on the decline. For example, a recent report from Hartford Seminary, based on a study of forty-one religious denominations, noted that churches that embrace contemporary worship styles are more likely to add new members. The fact remains that many churches and denominations continue to lack understanding of the changing generational waves and are suffering decline due to an inability to reach the younger generations.

2. *Fewer recruits for missions with a resulting loss of influence on unreached peoples.* Immediately following World War II, missionaries were recruited and sent to foreign fields in large numbers. Most were in their twenties and thirties and today have retired and returned home. This changing of the guard is forcing missionary organizations to face the future. It is apparent that most members of the younger generations are not attracted to serve as career missionaries nor do they financially support foreign missions as their parents did. While mission agencies are developing new methodologies to attract younger people to missions, they must keep generational dynamics in mind.

3. *Less money with which to finance missions or other local church ministries.* The "Fund-Raising Institute Monthly Portfolio" reports that people between the ages of thirty-five and forty-nine make appreciably more financial gifts to nonprofit groups than any other age group.[5] These thirty-five to forty-nine year olds are Boomers and older Busters. If churches do not make an effort to understand what motivates giving in the younger generations, it will certainly result in a loss of financial support for our churches. Younger people are not as motivated by duty as the Builders are. They must believe in the cause they contribute to and be able to see clear results from their investment.

4. *A continual trend toward the liberal agenda in the United States.* While the younger generations appear to be returning to a neotraditional lifestyle, they will likely support many liberal social issues, such as gay rights, abortion-on-demand, and the ultra separation of church and state. If we hope to command any Christian authority in the boardrooms of our government, schools, and businesses through the twenty-first century, it is vital that we reach a significant number of people in the new generational waves, people who will be the decision makers for our country for the next one hundred years.

5. *An inability to fulfill our God-given purpose to "make disciples of all the nations" (Matt. 28:19).* Since World War II more than 200 million people have been born in the United States. These are people for whom Christ died. If we estimate that 40 percent of them attend church on a given Sunday morning, some 120 million are candidates for new life in Christ. It is essential that we learn how to relate to these people so that we will be better prepared to follow in Jesus' steps to seek and save the lost (Luke 19:10).

Acts 13:36 is our example to follow. "For David, after he *had served the purpose of God in his own generation,* fell asleep, and was laid among his fathers, and underwent decay." The two phrases "served the purpose of God" and "in his own generation" clarify God's directions for ministry in a time of generational change.

The Purpose of God	Our Generation
Eternal	Temporal
Foundational	Cultural
Unchanging	Changeable

David understood his call to serve God's unchanging purpose among a particular generation in a changing generational scene. Ultimately the reason we must seek to understand the changing generational waves is related to God's call and command to us as believers. We are to serve his eternal and timeless purpose in a timely manner among a temporal generation.

Surviving the Riptides of Change

I am fascinated with oceans. I grew up in Colorado and never saw an ocean until I visited California as a tourist when I was nineteen years old. I can still remember that cold March day when I first looked on the seemingly never ending expanse of the Pacific Ocean and went for a swim. It had been raining in California for about two weeks, and the water was rough and extremely cold. After swimming for about thirty minutes, I noticed that my knee was so stiff from the cold that I could not bend it at all. I came back on shore, and as I was attempting to get warm, a native Californian walked by and said, "You must be a tourist." I responded that I was and asked how he knew. He replied that only tourists went in the Pacific Ocean in March when it is bitter cold and the riptides so treacherous. I knew what he meant by cold (it took almost an hour before I could bend my knee completely), but I had never heard of riptides.

Riptides, I have discovered, result when the return flow of the tide moves away from the shore. The resulting undercurrent can pull with great force back out to the ocean whatever it catches. The larger the wave, the stronger the riptide will be.

Generational waves can collide in a kind of riptide. As the seventy-six-million–member Boomer wave converges with the Builder wave and crashes into the Buster and Bridger wave, numerous problems emerge.

Not only are these generational waves creating turbulence in our society, they are also causing turbulence in our churches. That is why it is essential to understand each generational wave and how it affects the other waves to effectively serve God's purpose today. Most of us are faced with the problem of ministering to a church that includes members of all four generational waves. We must try to understand the generations as well as how they affect each other.

Part 1

The Builder
Wave

What Shaped the Builders? 1

Most of us have never heard of Dorothy Anderson Tormoehlen. She was hardly known outside her small Indiana community. Yet at one time her image was one of the most familiar in the United States. She was the Morton Salt girl. There were actually several Morton Salt girls over the years, but Dorothy was the one with the pretty yellow dress and the ribbon in her hair, found on containers in the 1920s and 1930s. As a niece of professional artist Mary Anderson, Dorothy was used regularly as a model for various renderings of children.

The Morton Salt Company began using a girl with an umbrella on their round, blue salt containers in 1914. Today, eighty-eight years later, the phrase "when it rains, it pours" continues to remind us of the philosophy of a generation that felt if you got one problem, you were going to get even more.

Three Groups of Builders

For the purposes of this book we will say the Builder generation is made up of people who were born prior to 1946 and includes some fifty-four million people or 19 percent of the U.S.

population. Various names have been coined to describe the Builders. Some describe them today: Suppies (senior, urban professionals), Opals (older people with active lifestyles), Rappies (retired, affluent professionals), Whoopies (well-heeled older people), and Grumpies (grown-up mature people).

Perhaps the most characteristic names are Strivers, Survivors, and Builders.[1] Whether as adults or children, Builders strived through World War I and World War II. They survived Black Tuesday, the Great Depression, and Pearl Harbor. Through tough times and with hard work, they built families, traditions, values, homes, friendships, communities, and churches.

We can divide the Builders into three smaller groups: the G.I. generation, the Silent generation, and the War Babies.

The G.I. Generation

The oldest Builders can be called the G.I. generation because they came of age and fought during World War I and World War II. Born prior to 1925, they are today over seventy-seven years old. There are approximately fourteen million people in the G.I. Generation representing 5 percent of the population. Seven presidents came from this G.I. generation. President George Bush was the last.

Some Famous G.I. Generation Builders		
Lloyd Bentsen, 81	Jimmy Carter, 78	J. D. Salinger, 83
Barbara Bush, 77	Oral Roberts, 84	Lena Horne, 85
George Bush, 78	Betty Ford, 84	Mike Wallace, 84
Paul Newman, 77	Andy Rooney, 82	Lady Bird Johnson, 90
Johnny Carson, 77	Billy Graham, 84	Norman Mailer, 79

Ages as of 2002

The Silent Generation

The Silent generation is comprised of people born between 1926 and 1939 who are between sixty-three and seventy-six years old in 2002. Approximately 25.6 million people in the

United States are currently in this age group, or 9 percent of the population. They are called the Silent generation because when they were in their prime, in the fifties, they were fairly content and silent, especially when compared to the G.I. generation. As a generation, they reached young adulthood during our country's years of prosperity in the 1950s. There was no need to be outspoken, so they tended to defend the status quo.

Some Influential Silent Generation Builders

Alan Alda, 66	James Earl Jones, 71	Della Reese, 70
Mel Brooks, 76	Quincy Jones, 69	Charles Robb, 63
Rosalyn Carter, 75	Walter Mondale, 74	Pat Robertson, 72
Jerry Falwell, 69	Colin Powell, 65	John Updike, 70

Ages as of 2002

The War Babies

People born between 1940 and 1945 were called War Babies. They represent about 5 percent of our total population or 14.5 million people. Today they are between the ages of fifty-seven and sixty-two years old.

Some Influential War Baby Builders

Joan Baez, 61	Aretha Franklin, 60	Geraldo Rivera, 59
Ed Bradley, 61	Jesse Jackson, 61	Diana Ross, 58
Dick Cheney, 61	Ted Koppel, 62	Diane Sawyer, 57
Angela Davis, 58	George Lucas, 58	Barbra Streisand, 60
Neil Diamond, 61	Paul McCartney, 60	

Ages as of 2002

Formative Experiences

Looked at as a whole, these Builder subgroups reflect common values and perceptions, which probably developed from the slower pace of life experienced in their formative years. Generally speaking, when the pace of change is relatively slow, succeeding generations are alike. Since the pace of change was not as rapid in the first half of the twentieth century as it was in the second half, these subgroups tend to share many characteristics.

As a generation moves through time and its members experience similar events, the members often begin to think, act, and feel in much the same way as other members of the generation.[2] What is taught and "caught" from parents, teachers, peers, and society contributes to the process. From early childhood each generation sees and interprets life events and experiences from within the context of the group. Over a period of time a particular generation becomes oriented to a particular way of thinking and perceiving. This process is called socialization.

The process of socialization begins at birth and continues into adulthood. A person's basic personality is formed by age four or five, but many of our preferences are actually determined during our late childhood and teenage years. The events that seem to have the most impact on people occur when they are between the ages of thirteen and twenty-two. The emotional responses to these events often stay with people for a lifetime, typically affecting two-thirds to three-fourths of people in a particular generation.

The good old days were different times for the various age groups within the Builders and very different from what Boomers, Busters, and Bridgers have experienced. For many it was a time when families met around the dinner table. Mom cooked. There was no pizza or McDonald's. Items were purchased for their value, not because they were trendy. People fixed things that were broken. They believed in God, country, and family. Most people were loyal, faithful, and dependable, and they were survivors.

Many significant events, inventions, and experiences occurred during the formative years of the Builder wave. The ones that follow seem to have been the most influential for most of the generation.

World War I

While only the very oldest of the Builders personally remember World War I, it is the beginning event of this generational wave. The Builders have fought in and supported more wars than any other generation in American history. World War I (1914–1918), often called the Great War and the war to end all wars, was the first truly global conflict. The United States tried to remain neutral, but with the sinking of the *Lusitania* (1915) and the beginning of unrestricted submarine warfare by Germany, the United States entered the war in 1917.

World War I is remembered for its four long years of trench warfare and the use of poisonous gas resulting in an estimated eight million troops killed. Hostilities were officially ended with the signing of the Treaty of Versailles. As American troops returned home, a new feeling of pride and hope resulted in a period of economic prosperity. The United States had been on the winning side of a global conflict, and everyone believed there would be no more wars.

The Roaring Twenties

The end of World War I ushered in a period of escapism called the Roaring Twenties (1921–1929). It was a time of prosperity when many Americans enjoyed a rise in the standard of living, fueled in part by overspeculation in the stock market and easy credit. The entertainment industry flourished as crowds flocked to theaters and sports stadiums. During Prohibition (1919–1933), many Americans broke the law by making liquor at home, and organized crime grew as gangsters bootlegged liquor. When investors overspeculated by purchasing stocks with money they did not have in hopes of reaping huge profits, stocks plunged, forcing individuals into bankruptcy and banks and businesses to fold. Massive agricultural, industrial, and financial problems led to the stock market crash of 1929, which took the roar out of the twenties.

The Great Depression

The stock market crash in 1929 was the beginning of the Great Depression, which continued through the 1930s. At the same time, dust storms resulting from drought and unwise farming methods caused severe damage, especially to farms in parts of Kansas, Nebraska, Texas, Oklahoma, and New Mexico. John Steinbeck's classic novel *The Grapes of Wrath* (1939) depicted the Okies' migration to California from the dust bowl of Oklahoma. More than fifteen million people were unemployed during the height of the Depression. Thousands lost their homes, mortgages on farms were foreclosed, and millions lost their personal savings.

The majority of the Builders living today personally recall the Depression era or have heard enough stories from their parents and grandparents to vicariously feel its effects. It is one of the primary socializing experiences of this generational wave and its impact cannot be overestimated.

Rural Lifestyle

The industrial age began pushing its way into the world of work about 1860, gradually beginning the process of making the Western world a powerful center of production. The rural lifestyle continued to play a major role in the socialization of the Builder generation, however, until about 1950. In 1900, 37 percent of the labor force was involved in agricultural labor, and this percentage slowly declined to 12 percent in 1950.

The farmer's main objective had to be survival. It took hard work, dedication, and prayer to overcome the natural ups and downs of nature, but there was a predictability to life, with the regular planting and harvesting cycles. The small-town atmosphere and slow pace allowed people to know, protect, and care for each other. Churches, schools, and family provided the necessary centers of social life.

The Automobile

Transportation was revolutionized during the lifetime of our oldest Builders as they grew up with the development of the automobile. Henry Ford (1863–1947) built his first car in 1896 and formed the Ford Motor Company in 1903. He pioneered mass production techniques, using an assembly line and standardized parts. This system was able to mass produce the Model T and dramatically lower the price of cars. To entice his own workers to purchase his product, he started paying workers five dollars a day. By 1929 his company had become one of the largest manufacturers of cars in the world.

A love affair with the automobile began during the Builder generation. Cars were simple and could be repaired by the average individual in his own driveway. But more important, the automobile provided a new form of expression for personal freedom and individualism on which Americans place a high value. Many youth learned to drive cars before age twelve, and no respectable boy, having reached the legal driving age, would fail to get his driver's license.

Radio

In the 1930s radio was new and began to capture the attention of the general public. For many Builder families radio was the main source of entertainment, and they became personal friends, if only over the air, with the likes of Edgar Bergen and Charlie McCarthy, Milton "Uncle Miltie" Berle, Eddie Cantor, Bud Abbott and Lou Costello, Fanny "Baby Snooks" Brice, and Bob Hope.

When Japan attacked Pearl Harbor and millions of young Americans were drafted, it meant giving up their favorite radio programs. Some became depressed because of it. By 1939 young recruits "were as addicted to radio as they are to television today."[3]

The military met the challenge by establishing the G.I. Network, which became the Armed Forces Radio and Television Service, to provide news, music, sports, comedians, and girls. One of the most popular shows was *Command Performance*, featuring stars requested by the G.I.s. The first show on March 8, 1942, featured Eddie Cantor, Dinah Shore, Danny Kaye, Merle Oberon, and a replay of the Joe Louis–Buddy Baer heavyweight fight.

The New Deal

At the Democratic National Convention of 1932, Franklin D. Roosevelt accepted his party's presidential nomination by declaring, "I pledge . . . myself to a new deal for the American people." Eventually *New Deal* became an umbrella term for a wide range of relief programs adopted to stimulate economic recovery from the Great Depression of the 1930s.

Many Builders remember the beginnings of organizations and programs such as the Securities and Exchange Commission (SEC), the Federal Deposit Insurance Corporation (FDIC), the Civilian Conservation Corps (CCC), the Civil Works Administration (CWA), and the Federal Emergency Relief Administration (FERA).

Although these organizations and programs did not actually end the Great Depression they did provide much needed relief for many people and, most important, communicated government's commitment to deal with America's economic woes.

Big Bands

During the big band era of the 1930s many dance bands became popular, such as the Dorsey Brothers Orchestra. Jimmy and Tommy Dorsey formed their band in 1934. Some of their popular songs are "Amapola," "So Rare," "Marie," and "I'll Never Smile Again." Later Frank Sinatra achieved stardom with Tommy Dorsey's band and had a mass following of teenagers in the 1940s that remained unequaled until Elvis Presley in the 1950s and the Beatles in the 1960s.

Benny Goodman, a clarinetist and bandleader, became known as the "king of swing." The Glenn Miller Orchestra played such songs as "Moonlight Serenade," "Tuxedo Junction," and "Chattanooga Choo Choo." Highly popular during the big band swing era, Glenn Miller dissolved his band in 1942 to lead the U.S. Army Air Force band in Europe and disappeared on a flight from England to Paris in 1944.

Other influential musicians included Louis "Satchmo" Armstrong, a jazz trumpet player and singer who originated scat, a type of improvised singing of meaningless syllables. He led a big band during the 1930s and 1940s and performed in films. William "Count" Basie formed his band in 1935 and performed in nightclubs, hotels, and theaters. His "One O'Clock Jump" is a jazz classic.

Other music styles helped to form Builder preferences. George Gershwin composed the popular concert piece *Rhapsody in Blue* (1924), musical comedies like *Funny Face* (1927) and *Of Thee I Sing* (1931), and the opera *Porgy and Bess* (1935).

Bing Crosby gained popularity through radio in the 1930s, entertained G.I.s during World War II, and eventually sold more than thirty million records, including the classic "White Christmas."

Pearl Harbor and World War II

On December 7, 1941, Pearl Harbor was the target of a surprise attack by the Japanese. Casualties included 18 ships sunk or damaged, 200 planes destroyed, and 2,323 servicemen killed. The attack spurred Congress to declare war on Japan, bringing the United States into World War II on December 8, 1941. Ask older Builders where they were when they heard that Pearl Harbor had been bombed, and most will be able to give you the exact place and time, so powerful was the impact of this event on the people of this generation.

The positive effect of Pearl Harbor was that it mobilized public opinion against the aggression of the Japanese and the Axis powers. World War II (1939–1945) once again brought an isolationist United States into a global conflict. The Builder wave pulled together as everyone did his or her part to win the war. Congress extended the draft to all men between twenty and forty-four years old. Men volunteered and were drafted into military service, women entered the workforce in record numbers, and those at home prayed and purchased war bonds in support of the war effort.

World War II created many heroes such as Gen. Dwight D. Eisenhower, Gen. Omar Bradley, Gen. Douglas MacArthur, Gen. George S. Patton, and Gen. George C. Marshall. Names like Midway, Iwo Jima, Corregidor, and Normandy bring back floods of memories to many Builders. The Normandy Invasion began on D day, June 6, 1944, and on May 1, 1945, Germany accepted unconditional surrender.

Harry S. Truman had become president following the death of Franklin D. Roosevelt, and on August 6, 1945, he ordered the atomic bomb dropped on Hiroshima and three days later on Nagasaki. Japan surrendered on August 15, 1945. The war ended, and our troops came home as victors from a war we believed we were destined to win. As some said, "God was on our side."

Rationing

During World War II rationing was used for the equitable distribution of scarce goods, and price controls helped limit inflation. There were twenty officially rationed items, including gasoline, sugar, meat, shoes, and tires. The Office of Price Administration issued stamps for commodities such as gasoline. Motorists were assigned window stickers with a priority ranking from A to E. Those who drove primarily for pleasure were issued an A sticker and could buy only two to five gallons of gas per week. Those with an E sticker—farmers, policemen, physicians, and drivers of emergency vehicles—could buy all the gas they wanted.

Stamps were issued for other rationed items. The number of stamps received depended on the number of people in the family. Some people gave or traded stamps to each other as needed, and all stamps had to be used by expiration dates to prevent hoarding. Early in the war, silk was diverted from the consumer industry to the war industry for the making of parachutes. When the silk supply from Japan was cut off, it was replaced by nylon. Women learned to mend their silk stockings, and nylon stockings became prized possessions.

The Korean War

From 1950 to 1953 the United States fought in the Korean War. This was the beginning of a new policy for containing

Communism. For many Builders fear of Communism escalated at this time and would prevail during the next couple of decades. After the Korean War reached a stalemate, an armistice was signed on July 27, 1953, with the thirty-eighth parallel becoming the border between North and South Korea.

Family, School, and Church

Builders remember a time when life was centered around the three big influences of life: family, school, and church. The process of becoming an adult was carefully supervised by these three institutions. Social activities revolved around the church and school. Family, school, and church most often worked together to build a fairly stable life, which helped people face difficult times and created a sense of unity. Couples rarely divorced. Few diversions meant that husbands and wives had time for each other. Most women did not work outside the home, so divorce, even in an unhappy marriage, was usually not an option for women. Traditional values permeated the home, community, and nation. Couples spent more time in childbearing and child rearing with fewer years to experience the "empty nest" or retirement.

Belief in God is taken for granted by most Builders, though, to many, religion means no more than that. To them we are "one nation under God," which means we do our duty to God and our country. Many remember when a day of public school opened with the Pledge of Allegiance and the Lord's Prayer.

Characteristics

Win and Charles Arn, writing about this generation in *Live Long and Love It*, say, "We were here before panty hose, drip-dry clothes, ice makers, dishwashers, clothes dryers, freezers, and electric blankets."[4] Builders were also born before the Pill, television, penicillin, polio shots, Frisbees, hula hoops, frozen foods, Dacron, Xerox, the Kinsey Report, radar, credit cards, ballpoint pens, tape decks, CDs, electric typewriters, and computers.

There is a danger in characterizing an entire generation with the broad brush strokes that follow. Of course, many people in a generation will not fit into such a description, but when the generation is taken as a whole it seems to exhibit these characteristics.

Hard Workers

As a group, Builders are hard workers. A rural lifestyle made this a necessity. Even with the emergence of the industrial age and the growth of factories and industry, hard work was required to survive in poor economic times. Labor laws were not strictly enforced, unions were just beginning to gain power, and working hard was the best way to keep your job and feed your family. Builders moved ahead due to diligence and perseverance.

Even Builders who have retired often continue to work hard. Common statements from Builders are, "I've got too many things to do" or "I'm busier in retirement than I was while working."

Savers

Sixty-one years ago Americans were learning to live with rationing and shortages in an effort to support the needs of World War II. It was a time of unity as everyone pitched in to support the Allied war effort. People got along. They adapted and learned to make something out of nothing. They found a way.

The Great Depression and the rationing of World War II taught Builders to save anything that might have value. You never knew when you might need that piece of string, used bar of soap, or piece of metal. The loss of money in the stock market crash and the bank closures created a desire to save money rather than spend it. Parents tried to save money to leave an estate to their children. A top priority was the future welfare of children.

Frugal

Luxuries were not available to most Builders until after the children left home, if then. During the lean years of the Depression adults and children learned frugality. Christmas mornings found stockings filled with nuts, apples, or oranges. Things were mended and repaired rather than thrown away—cardboard often stretched the life of shoes. Lights were turned out, heat was turned down, and energy-burning items were turned off to save money. In those days Builders used public transportation or walked to nearby stores. They planted gardens and canned food. Charging purchases on credit was not widely practiced. "Use it up; thin it out; make it last; do without" and "Make do or do without" were common sayings. Today Builders still tend to be frugal.

Patriotic

Many Builders fought in at least one war and are very patriotic. During the world wars the personal sacrifice required by all those who remained at home also created strong patriotic feelings. Holidays are important, particularly those having to do with patriotic themes, such as Veterans Day, Independence Day, and Memorial Day. Builders love and zealously support their country, its leaders, and its ideals. This meant that Builders in general found it difficult to be sympathetic with Baby Boomers who fled the country to avoid the draft during the Vietnam War or burned draft cards and flags in the streets.

Loyal

Commitment is highly valued by Builders. They united together to win the greatest wars ever experienced. They worked together as families to make it through the Great Depression. They still debate theological issues and defend their religion. They "buy American." Builders often worked for only one company for a lifetime, often on the same job. They trust the company, union, or government to take care of them for a lifetime.

Builders often see things as black and white rather than in grays. They do things because they believe it is right to do them.

Private

"We don't air our dirty laundry in public" was a regular admonishment from Builder parents to their Boomer children. "Good company, good food, good night!" was another saying that stressed the need for privacy.

Builders like the idea of knowing about people but resist sharing deep concerns that would allow them to really know each other. Small groups for Bible study are fine but not for personal sharing of deep hurts or needs. Such sharing is only acceptable within the family. Topics of a personal or intimate nature are taboo. Even between husband and wife, personal expressions of a sexual nature are not for public display. As Builder children were growing up, there were few physical expressions of love. Many Builders, especially sons, never received a hug or experienced closeness with their fathers.

Cautious

The times of simply surviving taught older Builders to settle for modest goals, hold on to savings, and be thankful for simply having a job. Few people were protected by life insurance, and the Depression stopped many from saving for retirement. Their lives were lived at the mercy of an unplanned economy and limited occupational opportunities. Luxuries had to wait until after the children left home, and even then, many Builders were too cautious to indulge.

Respectful

During their formative years most Builders were taught to have respect for people. Children were taught to respect their parents and elders. Workers respected their bosses. Privates in the military respected their officers. The position was respected even if the individual in the position was not.

As a result, Builders tend to be more thoughtful, considerate, and kind to others than the succeeding generations. Theirs is not a "me" generation as much as a "we" generation. They go out of their way to help neighbors and support each other in times of need.

Dependable

Builders see value in self-discipline, sticking together, and staying with the task in the face of any adversity. "If the job is worth doing, it's worth doing well," is their motto. Builders have continued to work hard even as the times have become more affluent.

Stable

For Builders who grew up in a rural lifestyle, life was fairly predictable. You rose early to do the chores. You cultivated, planted, watered, cultivated some more, and waited for the harvest, which eventually came. You planted and harvested at about the same times every year.

Certainly life was unpredictable in terms of the Depression and war, but in the things closer to home, such as family, work, and church, things were the same. As the times have changed and life has become more unpredictable, Builders try to remain stable, holding to the same goals and ideals their generation has valued for years.

Intolerant

As a group, Builders tend to be less tolerant than the Boomers, Busters, or Bridgers of people who are different from them. This is partly due to the fact that most Builders have spent most of their lives in fairly homogeneous communities. They have resisted change, believing the way they and their parents have done things is the best way.

Conclusion

For Builders, hard work, self-discipline, and sacrifice have paid off. They survived the difficult years of war and economic depression and believe that the affluence of the 1950s and 1960s proved that striving and surviving were the right way to go.

Today in the United States many Builders are retired, but a large number are still involved in some type of part-time employment or volunteer work. Joseph F. Quinn, a professor at Boston College, reported in 1998 that 30 percent of American men aged 65–69 and nearly 20 percent of women in that age group are continuing to work in some type of employment.[5]

Because Builders tend to be thrifty, many have substantial savings that allow them to live in retirement quite comfortably. Retirement plans and social security also help provide financial security. These Builders tend to travel extensively, enjoying cruises and tours with others their age. Some live part of the year in the northern United States and move south during the cold winter months.

Even though our bodies become less durable with age, because of medical advances and good health care, many older Builders enjoy good health. Some, of course, suffer from chronic illness, which may inhibit their ability to get around easily and care for themselves.

As we consider Builders, we must include those who do not have sufficient financial resources to live comfortably. Many of these senior citizens are forced to struggle daily to make their financial resources meet their basic needs. They fear losing their homes or needing expensive medical care. Many have lost a spouse through death and suffer the shock and loneliness of being alone after many years of married life.

"When it rains, it pours" became a watchword for the Builder generation. The Morton Salt girl's prophecy was fulfilled in several dramatic ways that continue to fashion the members of this generation.

While generational change is taking place, wise church leaders will continue to provide effective ministry to this powerful generation.

Builders and the Church   2

In his old age, John Quincy Adams illustrated that age is more a part of the mind than of the body. One day while Mr. Adams was walking slowly down a Boston street, a friend stopped and asked him, "And how is John Quincy Adams today?" "Thank you," replied the former president. "John Quincy Adams is well, quite well, I thank you. But the house in which he lives at present is becoming quite dilapidated. It is tottering upon its foundations. Time and the seasons have nearly destroyed it. Its roof is pretty worn out. Its walls are much shattered, and it trembles with every wind. The old tenement is becoming almost uninhabitable, and I think John Quincy Adams will have to move out of it soon. But he himself is quite well, quite well."[1]

Some people use three categories to describe the Builder generation: go-goes, slow-goes, or no-goes. Most, of course, are very much in the go-go category and are able and willing to support a church's ministry. They continue to have ownership of many areas of church life, particularly in the smaller church. Even though many Builders are open to change, a significant number will exercise their power as needed to keep things the same. Since Builder influence will continue to be felt in churches due to the networks of relationships and the informal influence exercised through them, it will be wise to understand what drives their ministry in the church.

This "make-do generation" has found faith, encouragement, and support during difficult times in their churches. In the first half of the twentieth century, churches were often found at the center of a town's social life. It is no accident that the churches of that era were found at the center of town. Their location was a physical statement of a true reality.

Builders who grew up in the 1940s and 1950s were trained to attend Sunday school and church, and for many of them this habit continues into the twenty-first century. If Builders do not attend church because of a spiritual commitment, they may attend because of a social commitment. Most Builders believe in God, with the percentage of atheists and agnostics lower in this generation than in the other three. According to research conducted by Dr. Thom Rainer at the Billy Graham School of Missions, Evangelism and Church Growth, 65 percent of Builders believe in Jesus Christ as their Savior.[2]

While Boomers, Busters, and Bridgers can be found in disproportionate numbers in larger churches, the Builders are most often found in small churches. Commitment to Christ means being a member of a church and supporting its activities, so the church has become central to their way of life. They believe that if they support the church's programs, the church will be successful, even if it is small.

Builders, then, have a strong sense of obligation to serve the church. They are often at the heart of their churches, in part due to their dedication and willingness to serve. They are the most churchgoing generation, and they give generously to charities—especially religious organizations.

The church's answer to ministry needs until the early 1970s was programs. If we needed to reach the lost, we had a week of revival. If we needed to reach out to those in other countries, we started a missions program. To carry out the goals of programs, committees and boards had to be created. Churches established during those years were often organized around a number of committees and boards, and people who showed particular interest in a special program were placed on a committee to oversee it. Thus the Sunday school had an education committee, the missions program had a missions committee, and the nursery had a nursery committee.

One of the main assumptions about ministry concerned knowledge of the Bible. Most believed that if anyone knew enough of the Bible, he or she would do the right thing. Bible study focused almost exclusively on learning the content of the Bible—Scripture memory associations sprang up for adults, and Bible quizzes became quite popular for children and youth.

A great deal of time was given to Bible study and prayer, and Builders did learn much about the Bible, but there was not always a lot of time given to defining their personal belief system. Many learned the words of the Bible without letting them penetrate their lives. Today Builders have a continued interest in Bible study and are often the teachers of Bible study groups.

Ministry through Foreign Missions

Following World War II the driving force in financial stewardship for Builders was missions. Returning G.I.s had seen new regions of the world. They had seen the results of sin in the Holocaust and the great need for Christ in the countries of Europe and Asia. The burst of missions and mission agencies immediately following World War II was fueled by economic growth and the willingness of Builders to financially support foreign missions.

Still today missionary efforts are heavily funded by Builders. This of course is to be lauded. Untold thousands, perhaps millions, of people have been brought into the kingdom of God through foreign missions. Yet for many Builders true ministry is defined only as missions. If ministry does not flow toward missions, it is of little use. Builders often say that a missions-giving church is a growing church, and that implies that a church's focus must be on worldwide missions. Though the result has been the growth of missions, it has often been at the expense of home-based ministry, which has sometimes meant a weakened home church. This eventually leads to less money being given to foreign missions.

Today Builders sometimes feel a need to defend their view of ministry, and they are slow to adopt any new way of doing church. Builders are usually satisfied with modest and plain church facilities. They may live, drive, and work in air conditioning, yet they resist putting air conditioning into their churches, feeling that such expenditures for the church building are too extravagant. Builders are hesitant to go into debt for church facilities or land purchases.

Many Builders have attended the same church for years. They have come to appreciate the songs, order of service, and decorations that have remained the same for a long time. Builders resist change in their churches because change destroys the stability and the security they expect. In making changes in a traditional church, care should be taken to affirm the validity of previous ministries, underscore the biblical basis of past ministries, present changes as an extension of the past, and move in a loving, accepting, and patient manner. As much as possible, when making changes in key ministry areas, it is wise to have two ministries—one in the new format and one in the style appreciated by the Builders. (See part 5 for information on how to make changes in the church without alienating Builders.)

Loyalty to Denominations

Usually Builders are strongly committed to their denomination or theological perspective. While younger generations change churches easily, Builders find it difficult to leave their church or denomination. They will support a church with problems or even a declining church, since they feel it would be disloyal to leave. Churches with strong denominational identities tend to hold on to their Builders even when they relocate. However, the same churches regularly lose many of their younger members to churches that offer greater choices or a more upbeat style of music.

For Builders, corporate worship is a time of quietness and contemplation of God. A worship service that requires minimal audience participation and that includes hymns, expository or content-oriented sermons, a pastoral prayer, recognition of guests, and organ/piano music is preferred.

Ministering to Builder Believers

Approximately 15 percent of church members today are Builders over the age of sixty-five. Some older Builders have given up their involvement in ministry, feeling that they are not needed anymore. Others no longer serve in churches, believing that they have done their time and now the younger generations should take over.

The truth is that many people have done their greatest work in old age. For example, former President Ronald Reagan served as president of the United States while in his seventies. While in their eighties Albert Schweitzer oversaw a hospital in Africa, Michelangelo designed the Church of Santa Maria degli Angeli, Winston Churchill wrote his four-volume *A History of the English-Speaking Peoples,* and Benjamin Franklin worked out a compromise that led to the ratification of the U.S. Constitution. Grandma Moses painted her first picture at age seventy-six, Colonel Sanders made his first million when in his seventies, Amos Alonzo Stagg did not retire from collegiate coaching until the age of eighty-three, and George Adamson of *Born Free* fame ran his primitive wildlife camp in eastern Kenya until his death at age eighty-three.[3]

While many churches have senior ministries, some churches tend to ignore older Builders, who still need the ministry of the church. Many have faithfully served Christ and his church in difficult times and still have much to offer in personal wisdom and active ministry. They are due our honor and respect.

The personal needs of younger Builders may be very different from those of older Builders, but all Builders seem to have

Need to effectively engage this group

some similar spiritual needs. Builders usually are not looking to their churches for entertainment, although they need and enjoy the socializing the church provides. Most Builders want to learn, grow, and serve in the church.

Aging may bring physical difficulties, but, for most, aging is in the mind more than in the body. "Individuals can be elderly at age fifty, or they can be young at age ninety."[4] "The thermostat of true aging is set by one's mind, by serenity of spirit, by continued growth, and by purposeful activity."[5]

Satchel Paige, the legendary baseball player, once asked, "How old would you be if you didn't know how old you are?"[6] His question points out the view of many gerontologists that old age is essentially a matter of the mind. Some Builders are recent retirees who are still full of energy. They will probably want to be involved in many activities. However, the older Builders may prefer less ministry involvement. For them, service to the church will need to be done in shorter chunks of time. Many have worked hard all their lives and will want to take long vacations during their retirement. Their ministry will need to be planned around their times of travel.

Here are a few ideas on how to keep Builders involved in their churches.

Group Activities

Builders may find that their families and friends have moved far away and live in other cities. Their need for meaningful relationships continues, and churches can provide groups, classes, and activities to help develop new relationships and maintain old ones. Builders like being with other Builders. Group activities built around tasks and trips will be the best attended. Try monthly luncheons or bimonthly trips.

Sunday School

Sunday school was the main ministry when many Builders were in their prime, and they still see it as the primary ministry of the church. The maturity and wisdom of Builders can be used more wisely than we have often done in the past. Consider using Builders in panel discussions and for teaching parenting classes, counseling young family members, leading Bible studies, and teaching new-believers or new-members classes.

Missions Projects

Builders usually provide strong financial support to the church, having established consistent habits of giving. Those who are enjoying financial security and who no longer have dependent children or grandchildren often give generously.

Their strong emotional tie to missions will continue, and churches should work with this by asking Builders to help fund short-term missions trips for Busters and Bridgers. Of course, they ought to be encouraged to go on short-term missions trips themselves.

In-Depth Bible Study

Builders enjoy classes on books of the Bible, theology, and eschatology. They also benefit from such classes as those on handling finances during retirement or restoring relationships with adult children or effective grandparenting.

Groups and classes that have as their objective personal growth may not be as attractive as ones that stress the learning of content, but they may be what Builders need most. Many Builders have grown up believing they should be reserved about their feelings as well as their faith. They may need to learn how to reach out to others and share their faith.

Focus on Marriage and Grandparenting

Many Builders have had happy or at least enduring marriages. Family, home, and marriage have been very important in their lives. Effective ministry to this generation must respect this focus by covering new family needs based on the Builders' life stage. Unfortunately, divorce among Builders is becoming more prevalent than in the past. Ministry to recently divorced people and to those whose spouses have died is essential.

Focus may also need to change to grandparenting at this time. A grandparent may have a wide range of concerns from simply being a good baby-sitter to knowing what discipline is appropriate. Churches should help Builders be good grandparents by providing counsel, classes, and resources. Builders who have had successful experiences in any of these areas can be used in teaching others.

A throng of Builders are finding that the term "unplanned parenthood" has a whole new meaning. Take the example of Oscar-winning actor George Kennedy who, at age seventy-five, along with his wife, Joan, age sixty-eight, adopted their five-year-old granddaughter, Taylor, in 2000.

Grandparents become parents again for several reasons. Their child may be unemployed, in jail, or abusive. In the last ten years, the fastest growing reason was alcohol and drug addiction among parents. When children are placed with grandparents because their parents have one or several of these problems, the children come with emotional, medical, and behavioral problems. This makes parenting the second time around difficult or next to impossible. As of March 2000, 3.9 million children were living in households headed by their grandparents. About one-third, or 1.3 million, are being raised by their grandparents alone. This number has increased 53 percent from 1990 to 1998, up 75 percent since 1970.[7] The positive side is that the child's well-being is taken care of and, of course, you cannot be old with a kid around. Grandparents in this situation, though, need the understanding and support the church can provide.

Contact with Other Generations

Builders should not relate in ministry only to other Builders. Effective programs have been built around the goal of intergenerational involvement. Even though relations between older Builders and Boomers were strained in the '60s, much of the animosity has dissipated, although some Builders still have not reconciled their differences with their Boomer children.

Builders often relate well to their grandchildren and great-grandchildren—the Busters and Bridgers. As we will see in chapters to come, the Busters and Bridgers are returning to values similar to those of their grandparents, and, as a result, strong bonds are developing between them and their Builder grandparents/great-grandparents.

In ministry this means two things. Churches should seek to bring Busters, Bridgers, and Builders together, and if there is tension between Builders and Boomers, attempts should be made to encourage reconciliation. Churches can provide a great service to all generations by providing forums for discussion and reconciliation.

Help with Retirement

Retirement means different things to different people. Some have said:

Retirement is what follows your midlife crisis.
Retirement is twice as much husband and half as much money.
Retirement comes just before senility.

A study by Dr. Don Anderson found that the thought of retirement evoked four major feelings—fantasy, fear, frustration, and fascination.[8] A few continue to see retirement as fantasy. They cannot even imagine what it is going to be like to not have to go to work each morning. However, most Builders now live in some stage of retirement. Others have great fears: fears relating to how they are going to live financially, selling a home, moving in with children or into a nursing home, or fear of death. Retirement is the last big phase of life through which we go before death. Some face retirement with a great deal of frustration. Perhaps there are goals they have never achieved, relationships that have not been healed, and missed opportunities they will never be able to retrieve. Some face retirement with anticipation of the possibilities before them—a part-time career in another field, time for a hobby or travel. In short, retirement is simply one phase of life. As such it leaves us with certain vulnerabilities, though it also offers many new opportunities.

One of every three retirees returns to work.[9] Their reasons are varied: to earn money, for social contact, or to fill empty hours. Most do not return to a forty-hour-a-week job but prefer to work part-time. A growing body of evidence suggests that those who work part-time are more likely to stay healthy. Providing information to businesses and Builders to assist in job placement is a service that many churches can provide their older members. Today life cannot be so neatly divided into stages of education, work, and retirement as once was the case. Once again, churches can provide ministry to help Builders cope with the changes.

Providing Avenues for Ministry

The complex issues facing individuals today make pastoral care one of the more difficult areas of ministry. Today's pastor cannot be an expert in every new area of personal need, but Builders can be trained in pastoral care. Their past experiences probably mean they will be able to love and be willing to listen to others. Studies have found that older people find it much easier to say "I love you" than young people and thus may be the best ones to extend their love through pastoral care. Using Builders in this way will extend pastoral care to a larger percentage of the church body. When a pastor is not available, Builders can be.

Encouraging an Acceptance of the Future Church

Many Builders have faithfully served God in their churches, but it is often true that their children, grandchildren, and great-grandchildren are not serving God and are not comfortable in the churches that Builders enjoy. We need to help Builders see that ministry must be formed and shaped with their grandchildren and great-grandchildren in mind. By being open to new ideas and new ways of doing ministry, Builders can help create churches to which these youngest generations will want to come. See part 5 for ideas on how this may be accomplished.

Conclusion

Gen. Douglas MacArthur had a plaque on his wall with the following statement about age: "Youth is not a time of life, it is a state of mind. You are as young as your faith, as old as your fear, as young as your hope, as old as your despair."[10]

Builders will find the aging process less traumatic if they find meaningful and challenging ways of using their time. Churches can have a major role in helping Builders find places of service.

Aging Builders   3

The writings of Allen G. Odell are legendary among Builders. He first began writing in 1925, and for almost four decades his short poems were seen and read at more than seven thousand locations in forty-five states. In the mid-1960s a set of his poems was placed in the Smithsonian Institution. His favorite poem was:

> Within this vale
> Of toil and sin
> Your head grows bald
> But not your chin
> . . . Burma Shave.

Allen's dad owned the Burma-Vita Company. In 1925 for two hundred dollars he put up the first Burma Shave signs himself in southern Minnesota. By 1948 the popular signs were gradually disappearing, victims of high speed travel and interstate highways. The signs were discontinued in 1963 after the company was sold to the Philip Morris Company.

Allen Odell was an ad man's gem. He understood his audience and communicated to them in a way that will be remembered for years to come. His Builder audience needs to hear greater words than those Burma Shave poems. At least 35 percent of them (twenty-one million) have a need to hear the saving words of salvation. As Builders continue to age, their time to hear and receive Christ is getting short. Many are open to the gospel and will listen and believe if churches reach out to them in appropriate ways. Serving the needs of aging Builders will develop openness and credibility in them so that they will be ready to hear the gospel at a later time.

Common Areas of Concern

Today's senior Americans have never had so many options for their retirement years and are living longer to enjoy it. Less than 10 percent of American seniors are actually living in total-care facilities. The great majority of Builders are living independent, active lives. In fact there is a growing trend toward what some call a "longevity revolution." As of September 1998 an estimated 66,000 Builders were older than 100 years (and in 2000 there were 4,259,000 people over 85). A Census Bureau study predicts a twelvefold increase in centenarians by 2050, to 834,000 persons! That is more people over the age of 100 than currently reside in Mesa, Arizona, or St. Petersburg, Florida, or Las Vegas, Nevada.

Only about 18 percent of centenarians are mobile and healthy, but medical experts predict that an increasing longevity and better health care will lead to healthier centenarians in the future.[1]

Aging does press its own set of unique needs into the lives of Builders, and churches can offer answers to spiritual concerns as well as help in other areas. Churches can help members through personal problems by responding in appropriate ways to their needs and by providing a wide range of participational options—personal, family, and social activities. Aging Builders will need the support of churches in the years ahead as they encounter some, if not all, of the following.

Financial Concerns

Many elderly Builders are living on fixed incomes. Whether it is social security or diminished income from investments, they have to struggle to live on their income, and many have had to live at a lower standard of living than they did when younger. Some elderly people, however, have been able to amass large estates, and they struggle to know what to do with their unexpected wealth.

In past years, retirees usually had to rely on a good savings account for their living. Today retirement income comes from a variety of sources. Knowing how to manage these funds can be a challenge for individual retirees. Churches can reach out to them by offering financial planning help or putting them in touch with agencies that can help.

Churches can teach older Builders how to recognize and avoid fraud. Unscrupulous people prey on the elderly with phony investment opportunities involving land sales, time shares, stocks and bonds, commodities and futures trading, gems, precious metals, franchises and distributorships, oil and gas, art, rare coins, financial planning services, and every other conceivable scam. The church can provide workshops to educate the elderly. For information, contact your local Better Business Bureau.

Affordable Housing

Housing issues are often problems for the elderly. They may have property to sell and decisions to make about what housing is affordable for them. It may be that people on fixed incomes would benefit from banding together in shared housing arrangements. Housing may be a particular problem for single seniors, and in today's society, divorce and widowhood create a longer period of living alone than used to be the case. Churches can assist with these problems by providing written resources, counseling, and classes. They may be able to set up networking to inform their senior members of affordable housing or roommates.

Personal Safety

Personal safety is and will continue to be a major concern for elderly Builders. Some elderly people who live alone carry beepers or cell phones to alert friends or neighbors that they have met with some mishap. The NRA offers a program on how to protect yourself without the use of firearms—the Refuse to Be a Victim course. Mainly for women, this three-hour seminar offers tips on home and personal security.

A church too can offer courses on personal safety and provide literature on the topic. Some churches may be able to train individuals to do safety checks on homes, giving ideas on how to make them safer.

Declining Health

In 1900 the average life expectancy was less than 50 years and only 4 percent of the population ever reached 65 years of age. By 1950 the average life expectancy was 68.2 years. Today the average life expectancy is 76 years and 12 percent of our population is 65 or older. By 2020 life expectancy will be 78.1 years. It is estimated that by 2040 life expectancy for males will be 87 years and 92 years for females.[2]

Today's Builders worry about their health. Many elderly Builders suffer from a variety of illnesses. Some studies have found that 85 percent of older Americans suffer from conditions that could be improved through better nutrition. Cited in the *Journal of the American Medical Association*, one study showed that half of independent individuals sixty-five years of age or older have specific nutritional deficiencies.[3]

To maintain good health, older Americans must have a nutritious diet and proper exercise. They should have regular medical checkups and have the resources to obtain needed medications and immunizations. When money is tight, however, food and medical care are often the areas where elderly Americans choose to scrimp.

Churches can help by providing their elderly members with hot meals or groceries, or they can help them find such services elsewhere. Transportation to clinics is a valuable service as well as exercise classes and workshops on nutrition. Church members with expertise could help the elderly understand and complete Medicare forms.

Adequate Transportation

It is a time of crisis in the life of an elderly Builder when he or she can no longer qualify for a driver's license. It is not only a loss of freedom to get around but an emotional loss as well because it puts one's competence into question. Without a driver's license an individual must rely on public transportation or family and friends. Public transportation is not always safe in larger cities, nor is it convenient. Many elderly people would prefer not to have to rely on family and friends for rides. Churches could provide regular transportation to grocery stores, malls, and clinics for the older Builders in their immediate community as a way to build relationships for greater ministry in the future.

Preparation for Death

No one likes to think about his or her own death. People approaching the end of their physical lives often go through denial and put off making important decisions until it is too late. Those who take the time to prepare for the end of life find that there are numerous benefits. When decisions are made concerning a will, a living trust, and burial preparations, the elderly person will have peace of mind that his or her wishes will be carried out. It also benefits the surviving family members by reducing the number of decisions that must be made at an emotional time.

Since many elderly people do not know where to start in making these preparations, churches can help by offering classes or workshops on wills, avoiding probate, living trusts, funerals, and funeral preparations. Assisting elderly Builders with physical preparations for death leads naturally into a discussion about spiritual preparation. It may be a time to lead some to the Lord and to help Christian seniors face death with the assurance of eternal life.

Spiritual Needs

Often as people age, they begin to think seriously about spiritual matters. Builders were taught not to share personal concerns in public, and many have avoided discussing such issues, but they may yearn to do so. Common Builder wisdom advised one not to discuss religion or politics, so churches must proceed with caution. Providing forums that deal with broad spiritual topics such as salvation, death, forgiveness, and eternal existence would be a good first step. If these are presented in a respectful, loving manner, follow-up may be possible. This could be done by appointment in Builders' homes, which would allow for further discussion on a personal level.

Use of Leisure Time

People who worked hard at a career may not have had the time or inclination to develop hobbies or other interests. Having never focused on interesting and healthy ways to occupy leisure hours, many Builders now spend too much time alone and watching television. Boredom is a major problem.

Churches can minister to their retired members by providing opportunities for them to get together during the week at Bible studies, exercise classes, trips to the library or museum, and the like. All Builders should be encouraged to help where they are able in church ministries. They can be involved in Vacation Bible School, day-care programs, and foster grandparent programs. They can tend the church library, plant flowers, or do visitation.

Sometimes retired people feel they are not needed and have trouble seeing where they can fit into church ministry. With a little encouragement, many will find areas of meaningful service and good ways to spend their time.

Substance Addiction

Loneliness often leads to drinking or other substance abuse, and alcoholism is as common among older Americans as it is among the younger. The addictions of Builders may go undetected since they do not have to go to work every day, do not usually commit crimes, and can stay at home for long periods. Builders do not talk about substance abuse, considering it a weakness to be ashamed of. They are, therefore, not likely to receive treatment.

This is another reason why churches must provide activities that will help older Builders get out of the house and build new relationships. Some churches may even be able to provide in-depth counseling. All should be able to refer their members to Christian counselors.

Elder Abuse

Elder abuse is a growing crime in the United States. Not as well understood as child abuse, it is a problem that is likely to gain much more publicity in the future as the general population continues to age.

Dr. Susan Lichtman, director of the Center for Aging Resources, defines elder abuse as "any action against a senior using violence or threat of violence against the senior's will."[4] Elder abuse often occurs when an older Builder lives with his or her children or grandchildren. It also happens in nursing homes and other elder-care facilities. Churches must speak out against abuse of any type. Making counseling or just a listening ear available may be helpful to the abused and the abuser.

Reaching Unchurched Builders

The changing structure of the family has left many Builders with weak support networks. "[Many] years ago," says Dr. Lichtman, "many people were in each generation, with few generations alive at a given time, sort of a flattened triangle. People had more children. Now, the family looks more like a bean pole, with multiple generations alive at any given time with few numbers in each generation."[5]

This change in the family structure is creating a need for caregiving with fewer caregivers available. This is an open door of opportunity for churches that wish to reach the Builder generation. Churches can meet the real needs of people who are hurting and at the same time reach this generation with the gospel of Jesus Christ. Here are some ideas.

Set Up a Hot Line

Consider offering a hot line service for people to call who need help. There are some national hot lines for Builders. By calling 800-955-7848, Builders can have answers to general health questions provided by the American Physical Therapy Association. Along with the practical advice, callers are sent the free brochure "Fitness, a Way of Life." See the resources section of this book for other helpful phone numbers.

A creative church can offer a similar hot line that would try to help callers with problems and questions on a variety of subjects. A number of different brochures on the same topics could be provided free for the asking. Churches are beginning to set up Care Networks via the Internet. About 12–15 percent of Builders are on-line and the number is growing every day. Interactive Builders are able to contact a caregiver by e-mail and receive helpful information on issues of concern.

Provide Support Groups

Family ties are crucial in times of crisis. A study reported in January 1993 found that when things are going well for Builders, children are relatively unimportant. However, when a crisis hits, such as deteriorating health or loss of a spouse, support from children is crucial to prevent depression. About 35 percent of elderly parents receive some sort of help from their children in the form of shopping, transportation, and household chores. Nearly 60 percent receive emotional support such as simply having someone to talk to.[6] Builders who have this family support have better mental health than those who do not.

Between 40 and 65 percent of our elderly do not receive the support they need from their children. The community may provide help in some areas, but it is often the emotional support that is left wanting. A church can form small groups for the elderly in the neighborhood that will provide time for talking, offering each other advice, and socializing.

Government health statistics report that more than sixty million people are actively involved in caring for an ailing loved one. The Administration on Aging of the U.S. Department of Health and Human Services reported in May 2001 that more than seven million households have an unpaid caregiver providing assistance on a daily basis to a family member.[7] Family members who care for elderly parents or grandparents need support. They need to know that someone else understands their frustrations. It is also helpful to know there is someone to call when they need a respite. A support group can meet these needs, providing a forum for airing frustrations and stepping in with practical help when needed.

It is likely beyond the ability of most churches to provide long-term respite for caregivers. However, it may be possible to offer assistance to free caregivers briefly for short-term breaks so that they may go on errands, shop, or simply enjoy time for themselves. There may be teenagers who would be interested in visiting an elderly Builder or who could help with errands and small chores around the home. Other church members may be able to offer assistance for housecleaning, companion care, and handyman service.

Schedule Traditional Activities

An interesting study of widows over fifty conducted by Sara Staats, a professor at Ohio State University, found that widows were satisfied with their lives and as optimistic about the future as married women in the same age group. One way widows adjusted to being alone was by developing a network of friends and activities to keep them active and occupied. The older widows were the most involved in social activities.[8]

Consider providing some traditional holiday activities for Builders who may be without the family support normally associated with holidays. The smell of Christmas trees, cider, spices, or Thanksgiving dinners will fill the air with nostalgia and stimulate memories of the past. By offering a place for Builders to gather around the traditional holiday sounds, smells, and activities, your church can provide a ministry to those who might not otherwise hear the Good News of Christ and his love.

Help with Social Security and Income Taxes

With each new year there are changes having to do with Social Security that may be difficult to understand. Perhaps there are people in your church who worked in the Social Security field or Medicare agency who could make it their ministry to keep up with the changes and work with individuals who need assistance.

You may also be able to provide assistance to the elderly with filing their income tax returns.

Sponsor Trips

An increasing number of older Americans are traveling. Longer life spans, healthier living, and large financial estates are making it possible for Builders to take trips throughout the world. Whether as individuals or as part of a travel club, Builders are seizing opportunities to travel to places they have dreamed of visiting.

Churches should consider using tourist trips as a means of ministry to unchurched Builders. Tourist trips could be scheduled with the express purpose of bringing Christian Builders and unchurched Builders together for one or two weeks. To be a ministry to nonbelievers, at least 50 percent of the people on the tour must be unchurched. The Christian Builders who go on the trip should be very relational and be coached in how to develop friendships that will continue on after the trip is finished. After the trip, the unchurched members of the tour should be invited to other appropriate events that will expose them to the gospel.

Offer Classes

Most Builders still like to learn. A clear example of this is the Elderhostel movement. Elderhostel, which began in 1975, has blossomed into an international educational program offered at more than two thousand locations. The minimum age is sixty, but spouses as young as fifty are allowed. Classes are offered on a wide variety of subjects from whittling to Civil War history.

There is no reason why churches cannot develop similar classes and activities as a means of building bridges to unchurched Builders. These classes can be taught by church members or by volunteers from the local community college or public school. If the classes are creative and touch on topics that interest older people, Builders will come and participate. Classes like these should have a nonchurchy feel with no preaching, prayer, or pressure exerted. The object of the classes is to make a contact that can lead to further ministry in the future.[9]

Offer Counseling

Builders, of course, go through the same struggles as everyone else. They may suffer through boredom, depression, and anxiety. Older Builders have particular concerns that may not touch younger members of the population. As they make the transition into the last decades of life they often experience many losses: loss of a spouse, loss of income, loss of prestige, loss of driver's license, loss of home, and loss of health. To weather all of this loss, Builders would benefit from the counseling that churches can provide.

A major decision for a Builder is when he or she should move to an apartment for senior citizens or even to a total-care facility. Counseling can help the people involved make the decision and can help the elderly person adjust to his or her new home.

Be a Clearinghouse

Even if your church cannot provide many of the services mentioned above, consider becoming a clearinghouse where people can call to get information and referrals. Find out where people can turn when in need. Are there sources of home-delivered meals, low-cost transportation, and counseling? How do they locate elder-care facilities, medical help, and other services? Compile information on support groups for the elderly and for family members who are caregivers. Discover where people may turn for answers about daily medications, finances, and volunteer work. After you have compiled as much helpful information as possible, advertise your availability as a clearinghouse of information for people to call. You should consider printing a small handout for free distribution as a service to people in your community.

Conclusion

Most people make commitments to Christ before they are adults. Believing in Christ with the faith of a little child becomes more difficult as one ages. A lifetime of ups and downs, broken relationships, and frustrated dreams makes it difficult for adults to freely consider the claims of Christ. Bob Saxe knows that churches can be effective in reaching Builders for Christ. As the recently retired pastor to seniors at Bear Valley Church in Lakewood, Colorado, he has helped create a ministry that reaches out to unchurched Builders through various need-meeting ministries, such as transportation, help with filing income taxes, or completing forms for Medicare. In so doing, the people at Bear Valley have put feet on Christ's promise to help lift the burden when he said, "Come to Me, all who are weary and heavy-laden, and I will give you rest" (Matt. 11:28). They have discovered that Builders can and do make personal commitments to Christ as they experience the love of Christ demonstrated in practical, hands-on ways by Christians.

The Builder Generation

Aliases	Strivers
	Survivors
	Suppies (senior, urban professionals)
	Opals (older people with active lifestyles)
	Rappies (retired, affluent professionals)
	The War Babies (born 1940–1945)
	G.I. generation
	Silent generation
	Seniors
Formative Years	1920s, 1930s, and 1940s
Formative Experiences	World War I
	Roaring Twenties
	Great Depression
	Rural lifestyle
	Automobile
	Radio
	New Deal
	Big bands
	Pearl Harbor and World War II
	Rationing
	Korean War
	Family, school, and church
Characteristics	Hard Workers
	Savers
	Frugal
	Patriotic
	Loyal
	Private
	Cautious
	Respectful
	Dependable
	Stable
	Intolerant
Religious Characteristics	Committed to church
	Support foreign missions
	Enjoy Bible study
	Loyal to denominations
	Minister out of duty
	Worship in reverence

Builder Ministry	Provide group activities
	Sunday school
	Mission projects
	In-depth Bible study
	Focus on marriage and grandparenting
	Encourage contact with other generations
	Help with retirement
	Provide avenues for ministry
	Challenge them to pass on leadership
Common Areas of Concern	Financial concerns
	Affordable housing
	Personal safety
	Declining health
	Adequate transportation
	Preparation for death
	Spiritual needs
	Use of leisure time
	Substance abuse education
	Elder abuse education
Reaching Unchurched Builders	Set up hot lines
	Provide support groups
	Schedule traditional activities
	Help with Social Security and income taxes
	Sponsor trips
	Offer classes
	Offer counseling
	Train for grandparenting
	Be a clearinghouse for Builder needs
	Offer respite care

Part 2

The Boomer
Wave

Who Are the Boomers?　4

The early boom of babies following World War II was at first not surprising. A rise in the birth rate after the "boys came home" was expected. Within a few years, however, the staggering growth of four million babies a year alerted observers that something different was taking place. One thing was certain—the babies just kept coming and coming and coming. Between 1954 and 1964, more than four million births were recorded in the United States each year. The large Boomer birth rate created a "pig-in-a-python effect." As one can see the bulge of a pig moving through the digestive tract of a python, so the Boomer wave can be observed moving through society.

Advertisers were the first to catch on to the Boomer wave, which today represents 26.5 percent of the U.S. population. Marketers targeted Boomers' parents, who desired to give their children what they themselves didn't have during the Great Depression. In 1958 alone more than one hundred million dollars worth of Davy Crockett paraphernalia and twenty million dollars worth of hula hoops were sold.

Boomers were the most educated generation in American history up to their time. They made heroes of John F. Kennedy and the Rev. Martin Luther King Jr. They rejoiced in the successes of NASA and the first men on the moon while struggling through the emotional ups and downs during the Vietnam War. They made a success of *American Bandstand* and the "Top Ten."

Of the four broad generations described in this book, the Boomers are the largest generation. They are the most studied, rebellious, independent, and affluent generation of the four. *Baby Boomer* technically refers to those people born between 1946 and 1964. In 2002 they are thirty-eight to fifty-six years old and the generation comprises approximately 74.5 million people (26.5 percent of the population).[1]

As with the other generations, Boomers are not one homogeneous whole. They are a collage of subgroups as indicated by the numerous names given to this influential generation. These names include Yuppies (young, urban professionals), Dinks (double income, no kids), Postwar Babies, and Postwar generation. The name New Collar workers is given to those in service-oriented jobs between the Yuppie and laboring ranks. Unnamed is a Boomer subpopulation of have-nots: unskilled workers, nonworking women with children, and heads of single-income households with incomes below poverty level.

A descriptive name for this generation is Challengers.[2] The sheer number of Boomers has made them a challenge. In the 1950s the nation's school systems were forced to build thousands of new school buildings to house this new generational wave that was moving into kindergarten. Thousands of new teachers had to be trained to teach them. They challenged the tastes and styles of music as they embraced the Beatles and invented new dances.

Boomer Births

Year	Births	Year	Births	Year	Births
1946	3,289,000	1953	3,902,000	1960	4,258,000
1947	3,000,000	1954	4,017,000	1961	4,268,000
1948	3,535,000	1955	4,047,000	1962	4,157,000
1949	3,581,000	1956	4,163,000	1963	4,098,000
1950	3,544,000	1957	4,255,000	1964	4,027,000
1951	3,751,000	1958	4,204,000		
1952	3,824,000	1959	4,249,000		

In the 1960s, when many of the Boomers were in their teens and twenties, they challenged the morals, rules, and traditions of their parents, schools, and the government. With strong protests against the war in Vietnam and in favor of civil rights for African Americans, this decade became known as the turbulent '60s.

Today this largest generation in the history of the United States challenges our nation's economy to provide them with jobs and health care. And by the year 2010 they will challenge the ability of the Social Security system to provide the retirement income toward which they will have contributed for nearly fifty years.

The Boomers are at once a generation of wide diversity and uncanny similarities. Many of them came of age in a time when the United States was moving from the industrial age to the information age. The rapid pace of change created a massive generation gap—unlike anything ever seen before—between Boomers and their Builder parents. The formative decades for Boomers were the 1950s, 1960s, and 1970s.

The Boomer generation can be divided into two primary groups: the Leading Edge—those born between 1946 and 1954—and the Trailing Edge[3]—those born between 1955 and 1964.

The Leading-Edge Boomers

There are roughly thirty-one million people who are Leading-Edge Boomers (LEBs). A vivid memory of many of these older Boomers is the gathering of two hundred thousand on the Washington Mall on August 28, 1963, when the Rev. Martin Luther King Jr. delivered an emotional plea for equality on the refrain "I have a dream." Leading-Edge Boomers were the leaders of change. These older Boomers cut their political teeth during a time of activism and optimism. Though still activists at heart, today they are concerned with saving for retirement, keeping and advancing in their jobs, paying off their mortgages, taking care of elderly parents, putting kids through college and graduate school, and helping children get started in life.

Some Influential Leading-Edge Boomers

George W. Bush, 55	Reggie Jackson, 56	Clarence Thomas, 54
Connie Chung, 56	Diane Keaton, 56	Donald Trump, 56
Bill Clinton, 56	Barbara Mandrell, 54	Denzel Washington, 48
Natalie Cole, 52	Dan Quayle, 55	Oprah Winfrey, 48
Andre Dawson, 48	Sylvester Stallone, 56	Stevie Wonder, 52

Ages as of 2002

The Trailing-Edge Boomers

The second half of the Boomer generation, born between 1955 and 1964, is called the Trailing Edge. Also labeled Generation Jones (www.generationjones.com), there are about 43.5 million in this group. The Trailing-Edge Boomers (TREBs) were too young to be involved in the activism of the '60s. The two key events in their lives during the 1970s were the national energy crisis and the resignation of President Nixon following the Watergate scandal. Today they are concerned with nourishing their careers, buying a home, seeing children finish high school and get into college, and in some cases, still raising younger children.

Several changes took place during 1954 and 1955 that separate the LEBs and TREBs. For example, 1954 was the first year that a majority of American households had television. Older Boomers actually spent their first formative years with very little TV. The polio vaccine was introduced in 1955, ending a disease that had terrified early Boomers. Polio had been eradicated by the time the later Boomers were in school, but they had other worries. As children they heard much about the dangers of environmental pollution.

Some Influential Trailing-Edge Boomers

Anita Baker, 44	Tom Cruise, 40	Spike Lee, 45
Charles Barkley, 39	Dave Dravecky, 46	John McEnroe, 43
LeVar Burton, 45	Kenny G, 46	Akeem Olajuwon, 39
Dana Carvey, 47	Michael Jordan, 39	Pam Shriver, 40
Kevin Costner, 47	Bill Laimbeer, 45	

Ages as of 2002

Alice Kahn, writing in the *San Francisco Chronicle,* states that "the nightmare of disease that haunted the LEBs' childhood ended with a triumph from science and technology. The nightmare of the dying planet that the TREBs were raised with continues unabated."[4]

The early Boomers got the best education. They had more opportunities for good jobs than did younger Boomers because they entered the workforce at a time when the U.S. economy was expanding. Of course, they also faced the stress of the draft, the Vietnam War, and social unrest. In contrast, the younger Boomers faced deteriorating public education, cutbacks in college programs, and fewer job opportunities. Perhaps because opportunities were not as plentiful for the TREBs as for the LEBs, TREBs seem to be more politically conservative.

Formative Experiences

The common self-awareness and sense of destiny among Boomers was created by the staggering impact of changes that took place during the 1950s, 1960s, and 1970s. Among the changes were several high-impact events, which bonded Boomers into a generation set apart. These experiences stand in stark contrast to those that Builders experienced. Builders entered the world during a time of slow economic growth and its resulting depression. They faced wars and hardships that formed the work ethic and commitment characteristic of their generation.

Older Boomers, on the other hand, entered the world feasting on the victories and rising affluence following World War II. They moved through the first half of their lives literally on a forty-year binge fueled by industrial and consumer production.

The following events, inventions, and experiences helped to form the basic characteristics of the Boomer generation.

Cold War

Cold War is a term coined to describe the hostility between the United States and the Soviet Union that endured from 1945 to 1989. It arose out of the failure of the two former allies to agree on the postwar restructuring of Europe and the Soviet Union's imposition of Communist governments on the nations of Eastern Europe.

As children, many Boomers lived in fear that the Communists would take over the world. The consequences of this were vague but terrible in their minds. Events such as the U-2 incident (1960), the Bay of Pigs invasion (1961), and the Cuban Missile Crisis (1962) reinforced these fears. Most of these events affected only the Leading-Edge Boomers and are just history to the TREBs. The Cold War ended with the fall of the Berlin Wall in 1989 and the collapse of the Soviet Union in 1991.

Television

In the 1950s there was a huge growth in the popularity of TV. In 1950 there were 3.9 million households with TV, growing to just over 30 million in 1955 and to 46 million in 1960. The growth in households with TV continued to escalate throughout the formative years of the Boomer wave. Its popularity and influence were evident when over 700 million people, the largest TV audience ever, watched the first men walk on the moon on July 20, 1969.

Programs like *Leave It to Beaver, Father Knows Best, Make Room for Daddy,* and *Ozzie and Harriet* were a few of the original shows that were popular during the early years of the Leading-Edge Boomers. Trailing-Edge Boomers growing up in the '70s watched programs that reflected the society of that era, such as *One Day at a Time.*

The growth of mass media, particularly television, has helped give the Boomers common interests and goals, even across economic lines. Dr. Ross Goldstein, a San Francisco psychologist and cofounder of Generation Insights, a consulting firm specializing in Boomer trends, says that similarities among Boomers are "partly because of the advent of television. It created a homogeneity in this generation that was unprecedented before."[5]

Economic Growth and Affluence

Builders grew up in difficult economic times. The Depression and World War II brought hard times that demanded sacrifice and a frugal lifestyle. In contrast, as Boomers grew up, they seemed to float along easily with a booming U.S. economy. Some of the reasons for the Baby Boom were the plentiful jobs and growing wages that allowed families to have and support more babies.

Cheryl Russell reports on the economic growth of the early 1950s: "Median family income increased by more than $5000 during the 1950s and by more than $6000 in the 1960s, even after adjusting for inflation. In comparison, median family income did not increase at all during the 1970s, when the baby boom generation came of age."[6]

As Boomers began to get married and start families the old system of breadwinner husband and homemaker wife began to break down. The increase in family income in the 1950s and 1960s was directly linked to that of the double-income family. It began to take two incomes to make ends meet. This move to a double-income family system forced a redefinition of marriage and family and stands as the most significant difference between the lifestyle of the Builders and that of the Boomers.

Education and Technological Growth

Following World War II educational opportunities expanded exactly at the time Boomers were born. The G.I. Bill opened education to thousands of returning soldiers from World War II, and education was heralded as the answer to society's ills. Boomers have known since they began reading *My Weekly Reader* that education was the pathway to success in life. It's interesting that it was at this time that education became what professor Irving Kristol describes as the "adversary culture." As education began to stress issues of diversity and individual rights, it unwittingly became adversarial to the family, the church, and some feel, the nation as a whole. For example, resulting from the stress on individual rights, children are now able to sue their parents. This implies that the individual is more important than the family group. Kristol notes, "It is hardly to be denied that the culture that educates us—the patterns of perception and thought our children absorb in their schools, at every level—is unfriendly (at the least) to the commercial civilization, the bourgeois civilization, within which most of us live and work."[7]

The growth of technology—particularly the transistor—transformed Boomer lifestyles. Nostalgic Boomers remember with fondness their first transistor radios, and Trailing-Edge Boomers remember the first video game—Pong—introduced in 1972 with sales of more than six thousand in its first year. The transistor literally changed our lifestyle, making possible everything from sophisticated kitchen appliances to automatic cameras, from digital watches to cars with transistorized ignitions.

The new technology produced new products that made life easier and more fun and improved products already available. More efficient automobiles and the construction of the nation's massive freeway system opened the way for the development of the suburbs. Automobile travel provided people a way to "see the USA in their Chevrolet," and the growth of airline travel literally brought the world closer to home.

Rock and Roll

Whereas Builders grew up on the sounds of swing and jazz, Boomers cut their musical teeth on the new music style called rock and roll. No one, of course, popularized this new music form more than Elvis Presley. He rose to stardom singing a blend of blues and country western music. His sideburns, mannerisms, and attitude created what has become a cultural phenomenon. Songs like "Heartbreak Hotel," "Don't Be Cruel," "Love Me Tender," and "All Shook Up," along with concerts, television appearances, and more than thirty movies, popularized a new style of music that continues to affect Boomer musical tastes. Other groups that Boomers remember include the Turtles, the Monkees, the Grateful Dead, and of course, the Beatles.

The climax of the rock generation's involvement with rock music came on August 15–17, 1969, when more than four hundred thousand people gathered at a farm in Bethel, New York, for a concert showcasing the most famous performers of the times, including Jefferson Airplane, the Who, Jimi Hendrix, and Janis Joplin. The event combined a mixture of music, Vietnam War protest, and "good vibrations." Heavily covered by the media, it was depicted in the movie *Woodstock* in 1970 and became somewhat of a legend for many Boomers.

Civil Rights Movement

In 1955 Martin Luther King Jr., a Baptist minister, led a successful bus boycott to protest racial segregation in Montgomery, Alabama. Inspired by Mahatma Gandhi's philosophy of nonviolent civil disobedience, King founded the Southern Christian Leadership Conference in 1957 to combat segregation and racism.

Awakening the conscience of the United States, similar protests continued through the sixties. In 1957 the Civil Rights Commission was established to protect the African American right to vote. Later, the Civil Rights Act of 1964 prohibited discrimination in voting, education, hiring, and promotion of workers and guaranteed equal access to hotels, restaurants, theaters, and other public facilities.

The six-day Watts riot, August 11–16, 1965, was caused by long-term racial tensions and sparked by charges of police brutality. It resulted in thirty-four deaths and more than one thousand injuries. Some two hundred businesses were destroyed and property damage was estimated at two hundred million dollars. The riot alerted Boomers to the fact that legislative acts could not change the basic character of the nation. The protests, marches, and speeches stirred up the inward desire for justice in the minds of college-age Boomers and drew them into the national civil rights movement.

The New Frontier

During his presidential election campaign of 1960, John F. Kennedy called for a new frontier that would provide for federal aid for education, Medicare, equal opportunity in employment, and advances in space exploration. His call cast a dream of hope to a young generation that was tired of the Cold War and fear of Communism.

Following a president who was like a grandfather, JFK came roaring into the White House with a beautiful wife and preschool children. This "Camelot" presidency inspired widespread idealism and created an illusion that was never to be reality. The youthfulness of the president's family was a model for youthfulness in the '60s.

Kennedy's resounding statement, "Ask not what your country can do for you; ask what you can do for your country," became the trumpet charge for one of the most successful aspects of the new frontier policies—the Peace Corps. An overseas volunteer program still in existence today, the Peace Corps recruits volunteers who serve at the request of developing countries, usually for two years, in fields such as education, health care, and agriculture. Its goals are to help people and developing countries obtain basic necessities, promote world peace, and improve relations between the United States and the people of other countries.

Space Race

In 1958 the National Aeronautics and Space Administration (NASA) was founded to supervise U.S. space flights and activities beyond the earth's atmosphere. The agency focused on research and the building and testing of spacecraft. Its accomplishments include the launching of hundreds of satellites and space probes and six successful moon landings.

As a part of JFK's new frontier, a mandate was given to place a man on the moon in the 1960s. NASA's crowning achievement occurred on July 20, 1969, when the Apollo 11 lunar module *Eagle* landed and Neil A. Armstrong first walked on the moon.

The landing highlighted the hopes of Boomers, which were immortalized in Armstrong's words: "That's one small step for man, one giant leap for mankind." He later planted an American flag and left a plaque that read, "Here men from the planet Earth first set foot upon the moon July 1969 A.D. We came in peace for all mankind."

Assassinations

Actor Michael Douglas was in college in California. Kevin Kline was in high school in St. Louis. Jane Fonda was in Paris, filming a movie. Singers Peter, Paul, and Mary were en route to Dallas to give a concert. All can recall precisely where they were and what they were doing on November 22, 1963, when they learned that President John F. Kennedy had been shot.

The impact of Kennedy's assassination on older Boomers was similar to that of Pearl Harbor on the Builder generation. Older members of the Boomer generation are still preoccupied with the president's assassination. In the 1990s, Oliver Stone's movie *JFK* sparked a resurgence of assassination lore and a search for new clues to a possible conspiracy behind President Kennedy's death.

Actually three assassinations tarnished Boomer hopes and dreams: Kennedy in 1963, Martin Luther King Jr. in April 1968, and Robert Kennedy in June 1968. These assassinations were instrumental in tempering Boomer optimism about improving our society. Especially for African American Boomers, King's assassination has had long-lasting effects.

Vietnam War and Kent State

Boomers grew up in a time of social, racial, and artistic upheaval, and no experience characterized their turmoil more than the Vietnam War. It was the longest war in which the United States has ever been engaged and the first in which we failed to achieve our goals.

Throughout the '60s popular demonstrations and political pressure to end the war mounted. Many Boomers in their twenties were strongly opposed to continued American involvement. "Tune in, turn on, and drop out" and "Hell, no, we won't go" were the battle cries.

Following Richard Nixon's announcement on April 30, 1970, of the invasion of Cambodia and the need to draft 150,000 more soldiers for the Vietnam War, protesters staged antiwar rallies at Kent State University in Ohio. Governor James Rhodes ordered National Guardsmen to the university, where they used tear gas to disperse the crowd. When a shot was heard, the Guardsmen opened fire on the unarmed students, killing four and wounding nine. The incident incited massive protests across the country.

Energy Crisis

The Arab-controlled Organization of Petroleum Exporting Countries (OPEC) imposed restrictions on the United States and other industrialized countries in retaliation for their support of Israel during the Yom Kippur War in 1973. The embargo caused gas shortages leading to rationing, long gas lines, and higher prices for petroleum products. A national speed limit of 55 mph was imposed to help reduce gas consumption. It signaled to the Boomers that there were in fact limits to the planet's resources. People began to realize that resources could not go on being depleted without severe consequences.

Watergate and the Nixon Resignation

In May 1973 the Watergate scandal unfolded. On June 17, 1972, five men had been arrested for breaking into the Democratic National Headquarters at the Watergate apartment and office complex in Washington, D.C. The intruders had been hired by the Committee to Reelect the President. President Richard M. Nixon denied any involvement, but investigative reporting by Bob Woodward and Carl Bernstein of the *Washington Post* implicated him and led to the events culminating in his resignation. (The reporters won the 1973 Pulitzer prize for their stories and wrote the best-seller *All the President's Men*, which was made into a film.)

On August 8, 1974, Nixon announced his resignation, becoming the first president to resign from office. Gerald Ford was sworn in as the new president the following day. He said, "Our long national nightmare is over," referring to the Watergate scandal. On September 8, 1974, President Ford pardoned Nixon for any crimes he may have committed in the Watergate affair. Many Boomers, because of policy decisions made concerning the Vietnam War, had begun to distrust American government. The Watergate scandal reinforced this lack of trust.

Characteristics

Like any large group of people, not all Boomers have the same beliefs or fit the same mold. Male and female, black and white, wealthy and poor, northern and southern Boomers may all have different views. The Leading-Edge Boomers tend to be the activists whose strongest formative memories focus on the assassinations of John Kennedy, Robert Kennedy, and Martin Luther King Jr.; the rise of the civil rights movement; and the Vietnam War. The Trailing-Edge Boomers were more strongly affected by the end of the war in Vietnam, Watergate, and the resignation of Richard M. Nixon. They cannot be rigidly grouped together. Yet there are some basic, valid characteristics that the members of this generation share.

Educated

Boomers attained the highest education levels of any generation up to their time. Nearly one quarter of them have earned a college degree, compared with only 9 percent of people over age sixty-five.[8] Changes in teaching methods and insights into the needs of all people affected the education of Boomers during their formative years. These changes have led to increased tolerance in all areas of race, gender, age, and belief systems. A major reason for differences between Boomers and Builders is the Boomers' higher level of education. Cheryl Russell explains in *100 Predictions for the Baby Boom* that education determines "the way people live, how they vote, what they buy, and what they believe. American society has become more diverse and more accepting of diversity because more of its members are educated. This is why the Baby Boom forges new ways of life and why there cannot be—no matter how much some people may want it—a return to the simple traditions of the past."[9]

An example of this diversity is seen in the people who represent us in Congress. Our congressmen used to be mostly white males over sixty. The impact of the Boomer generation is that members of Congress are now of diverse ages and races, both male and female. Paul Light of the University of Minnesota says, "As Boomers move through middle age they will likely continue to be more socially liberal than their Builder parents but will grow more conservative on the issues of crime and safety."[10]

Media-Oriented

For better or worse, Boomers are the first generation to be raised on TV. This nonstop influence united Boomers by a common "electronic" bond. Television shaped Boomers' values, turning them into a consumer market. Shows like *I Love Lucy, The Honeymooners, The Mickey Mouse Club,* and *American Bandstand* all provided common symbols, fads, and experiences unknown in times past.

During the Boomers' formative years, money spent on TV advertising soared from 171 million dollars in 1950 to more than 1.6 billion dollars in 1960, increasing to 3.6 billion dollars in 1970! By the time Leading-Edge Boomers reached eighteen, they had watched nearly 300,000 hours of commercials.

Radio also continued to have influence, primarily as a medium for music. Because radio programming is narrowly targeted to meet every musical taste, it still reaches Boomers today. They are not unlike other age groups who like radio because it holds their attention, moving quickly from one song to the next. It also costs less than other mediums and offers the freedom of listening while doing other things.[11]

Independent

Rapid changes during the information age taught Boomers that long-term relationships and commitment were going to be difficult to manage. Whereas their Builder parents may have grown up, gone to school, worked, and retired in the same town or geographical area, it has not been so for Boomers. Some Boomers stayed put during their childhood years, but they often went out of state for college or university. After graduating from college a Boomer often accepted a job in an entirely different geographic area. Once employed, many followed the legendary IBM (I've Been Moved) path to promotion. During the 1980s, when Boomers were working their way up the ladders of success, 17.3 percent of the general population moved every year. Of the major age groups, those that moved the most were those twenty to twenty-nine and thirty to forty-four years old, or almost all Boomers. The average person moved once every three to five years during the 1970s and 1980s. Today, of course, there continues to be great mobility in our society, but it has slowed down since the '70s and '80s. IBM is now allowing its employees to remain in one location longer than was common in the fast-paced '80s.

For Boomers, mobility destroyed the normal networks of relationships and commitments that are usually nurtured through many years of association. Many Boomers have not known the support of continuing relationships. They miss the commitments to church and work enjoyed by their parents. As they live through midlife they are feeling the need for friends and supportive networks. The years of having to uproot and separate from friends and personal commitments have taught them to hold long-term relationships and memberships at arm's length. For example, Boomers may join a health club a month at a time but rarely for a year or more. Similarly, some Boomers move from one church to another without concern. Boomers are independent and tend to be less loyal than Builders to an employer or even to a church. Most vote for a person, not a party.

Fifty years ago, people who were dissatisfied with their career choices simply accepted their lot in life. They stayed with ill-fitting jobs, earned their twenty-five-year pins or gold watch, and retired. Not so for Boomers. The idea of working twenty-five to thirty years for a gold watch is gone. Most Boomers will experience three to six major career changes during their working years.

Cause-Oriented

The formative years of older Boomers were filled with causes. Whether it was fighting Communism or marching for civil rights, protesting the war in Vietnam or volunteering for the Peace Corps, they pitched in and fought for what they believed in. Today Boomers are well represented in groups like MADD (Mothers Against Drunk Drivers), and they support such varied efforts as gay rights, pro-life, and preservation of the environment. Boomers still believe they must try to make the world better for everyone.

Fitness Conscious

As Boomers have aged, many have tried to stay in good physical shape. They patronize health clubs and health food restaurants. Since the 1980s they have caused the sales of muscle-building machines like Nautilus to grow and they have taken up swimming, tennis, and even tai chi in efforts to keep in shape.

There are far more recreational opportunities now than there were fifty years ago, and Boomers tend to enjoy participating in them. Hang gliding, indoor soccer, and sailboarding are just a few examples.

Rock Music Fans

Boomers still like music with a beat. The midlife resurgence of singers like Paul McCartney of the Beatles and Paul Simon and groups like the Moody Blues and the Beach Boys is directly related to the support of their aging Boomer fans.

As Boomers mature, they are broadening their musical tastes, but they are not likely to give up the music they have enjoyed for over a quarter of a century. One style of music that is attracting a larger Boomer audience is country music. Many Boomers also enjoy the same music as their Buster and Bridger children. Boomers are least likely to listen to the two formats of big band/nostalgia and easy listening/beautiful music.[12]

Activists

An advertising brochure for the American Association of Boomers declares, "We are the generation that makes a difference." It begins with an open letter that reads in part, "When we were younger, we wanted to make a difference. Some of us worked within the system. Some of us fought against it. But we all wanted to make a difference. . . . We can make a difference." Boomers are activists. They still like to get involved, whether as part owners of the firms they work for or on the school board.

Quality Conscious

Boomers were given practically everything they wanted by parents who desired them to have what "we never had." Targeted by every major manufacturer and marketer for the past five decades, Boomers are used to quality products. The affluent '50s and '60s created a craving, even a feeling of entitlement, for nice things. It does not matter whether it is cars, homes, or food; it has to be the best. Their children, the Baby Boomlet, contributed to the growth of private schools in part because Boomer parents desire quality education for their children.

Questioners of Authority

Due to the training they received from home, church, and the military, Builders rarely questioned authority. Boomers, on the other hand, learned not to trust authority. The Vietnam War and Watergate scandal taught Boomers to distrust government, the military, and other forms of authority. In the '60s they used to say, "Don't trust anyone over thirty." All Boomers are now over thirty, but they still find it hard to trust, being especially critical of politicians and people in authority.

Conclusion

Boomers have influenced our world since they first came on the scene. Think of the impact these Boomers have had: Bill Clinton, Reggie Jackson, and Sylvester Stallone, to name a few. In the 1950s Boomers rode the waves of victory flowing from World War II and a growing economy. Then in the 1960s they enjoyed a "Camelot" dreamworld complete with hopes for world peace and brotherhood. By the 1970s they were retreating as the wall of Camelot came tumbling down into piles of disillusionment and cynicism. During the 1980s they worked hard to establish their careers. They sailed through the 1990s enjoying the rapid growth of the stock market. In the twenty-first century the collapse of the technology boom makes Boomers wonder what the future holds and how they will fare in the years to come when it looks as though there will be less money, more crime, more pollution, and uncertain retirement.

Boomer Believers   5

A s we enter the new millennium, we face a new era in human history. Unless Christ returns this decade, the twenty-first century is not likely to be one of peace, prosperity, and justice. But it will be one of great opportunity for Christ's church.

The Lead Generation

Baby Boomers are members of what sociologists call the "lead generation." A lead generation tends to set the agenda for the entire nation. As the lead generation goes, so goes the nation—and the church. Local churches that are able to anticipate future directions and create solid strategies will experience growth. Those that do not foresee and adapt to meet this challenge will find it increasingly difficult to minister effectively. The Boomer population in the United States alone is almost three times the population of Canada. Churches cannot afford to ignore them.

Writing a decade ago about the need for churches to understand and minister to Boomers, Dr. Elmer Towns reminds us that "the Boomer influence must be faced by the church. Within ten years they will take over the leadership of local churches and denominational headquarters." He continues, "When they take over the leadership of Christian organizations, they will functionally operate the church differently. To properly reach them, we must recognize the unique needs they bring to Christianity. Just as the church cannot reach the Chinese without understanding Chinese culture, values, and language, so the church must understand the Boomer in order to develop a cross-cultural strategy to reach and minister to the Baby Boomers in America."[1] It is now over a decade later and we can see that much of what Elmer Towns suggested has taken place.

Some churches have found it difficult to attract and keep Boomers. Lyle Schaller was one of the first people to note the fact that churches were losing the Boomer generation. In an insightful article, "Whatever Happened to the Baby Boomers?" Schaller noted that "13 percent of the persons born in the 1955–64 era, the peak of the Baby Boom years, claim 'no church affiliation.' This contrasts to only 4 percent for those born in 1940 or earlier."[2]

A survey conducted between 1988 and 1992 by Dr. Wade Clark Roof, the J. F. Rowny Professor of Religion and Society at the University of California in Santa Barbara, was published in *A Generation of Seekers*.[3] Among other things, he discovered that of the seventy-six million Boomers about a third (twenty-five million) never quit going to church. Of the two-thirds that did drop out of church, close to 40 percent have returned. Putting both of these groups together, there are roughly forty-five million Boomers who are members of churches today. And of them about 58 percent, or twenty-six million, attend a church or synagogue on a regular basis. Not all, of course, attend Bible-believing churches. Dr. Roof divides these church attenders into two groups: "seekers" and "believers but not belongers." He found that 28 percent of all Boomers are believers and 9 percent seekers who hop from faith to faith. Only 4 percent of Boomers say they are agnostics and 1 percent atheists.[4] In the study mentioned earlier by Dr. Thom S. Rainer, it was discovered that 35 percent of Boomers in 1997 were believers in Jesus Christ.

Boomers and Religion

The spiritual economy in the United States is changing just like its fiscal economy. As the '60s generation matures, the Boomers' religious expression is more eclectic than ever. Throughout most of their lives many have simply ignored the church. While they may value it for its occasional social calls for justice, they have used the church primarily for hatching (baby dedications), matching (weddings), patching (counseling), and dispatching (funerals).

There are, however, some general religious perspectives around which churches can build ministries that will attract Boomers.

Commitment to Relationships

Boomers are sometimes characterized as uncommitted to church. Their interpersonal relationships tend to be weak, resulting in a high divorce rate and broken families, and they resist joining organizations. These factors mean that Boomers relate to the church differently than their parents did. The Me generation wants a personal relationship with God, not a set of rules. Corporately they want relationships with each other that are based on open and honest understanding of how people think and feel.

In practice the Builder generation's commitment to Christ was expressed through involvement with the institutional church. They gave their time, energy, and money to church. A common statement heard from Builders is, "Whenever the doors of the church were open, we were there." In contrast, Boomers see their commitment to Christ as a personal thing, not measured by church attendance. Both generations may be equally committed to Christ, but Builders tend to interpret commitment to Christ as equal to church attendance. Many Boomers believe that their church attendance does not reflect the degree of their commitment to Christ.

Church Membership

The independence of Boomers is evident in the way they change their religious affiliation. While Builders tend to remain committed to the denomination of their youth, many Boomers have changed religious affiliation at least once. According to a poll conducted by the Princeton Religion Research Center, "Nearly 25 percent of U.S. adults have changed their religious affiliation at least once, with conversion to Protestantism being nine times more common than conversions to Catholicism." Reportedly, 19 percent left Baptist churches, 11 percent left Methodist churches, and 6 percent left Presbyterian churches.[5] Many researchers have noted that most of those who change churches appear to be Boomers. Since Boomers often move easily from one denomination to another, people are seeing less value in denominational names than they did before. Many churches decide not to use their denominational name in signs and public advertising.

One of the reasons Boomers often do not follow in their parents' footsteps in choosing a church is because they are more mobile, moving on the average of once every three to five years with only about a fifty-fifty chance of attending a church of the same denomination they left. Boomers are attracted to churches that have celebrative and participative worship services with contemporary music. The church has become for them a way station or stopover on their spiritual pilgrimage.

People Not Programs

A general misconception surrounding Boomers is that they will not contribute money to a church. On the contrary, Boomers are not as egocentric as one might assume. Like all generations, as Boomers have aged, they have substantially increased their giving to charitable organizations, and now they are entering their peak earning years. Many are also inheriting money from Builder parents.

Perhaps because they are better educated, Boomers are sophisticated in handling money and tend to think carefully before investing it. Since they are concerned for causes and are highly relational, they want to give money to organizations that prove they are actually doing something of great value for people. They look for a return on their investment and want to see it firsthand.

In the church this is seen in the desire of Boomers to support projects and people who are close to home, since it is easier to see results in local ministries. It also means Boomers are more likely to give financially to ministry that effectively communicates a clear mission and strong vision (a big cause).

Living Their Faith

Boomers appreciate those who honestly live their faith as opposed to just wearing it on Sundays. They tend to be down-to-earth and think nothing of calling their pastor by his first name or wearing jeans and tennis shoes to church.

Boomers favor activism. They want to get involved and are usually open to ministry in the local church. They view themselves as problem solvers, but they will not minister purely out of a sense of duty or responsibility. They are just too busy for that. Ministry must fit their interests, needs, and sense of fulfillment. "Boomers are looking for action," writes Dr. Roof. "They are also looking for an identity, and churches with clear-cut beliefs and boundaries are best able to supply that."[6] They want vitality and movement in the institutions they participate in, especially the church. Often large churches that have a lot going on meet these needs because the participants sense that ministry is happening.

Experimenting

Much of the Leading-Edge Boomers' time in the '60s was spent experimenting—with drugs, causes, communes, and music. Many have also experimented with religion, trying out Eastern religions, EST, self-help philosophies, and New Age cults. Those who are Christians bring their desire to experiment to the worship service. They have enjoyed singing and clapping to praise songs and bringing drama and dance into the service. Hugs and high-five affirmations are often enjoyed by this generation.

Tolerant of Differences

During the first fifty years of the twentieth century, people tended to see everything as either black or white, true or false, pure or impure. There was no in-between. Boomers in general tend to see things in shades of gray rather than in black and white. They seem to have a greater tolerance for different viewpoints, lifestyles, and ideals. In the *Christian Education Journal,* pastor Leith Anderson writes, "Especially frustrating to many senior pastors is the Baby Boomer's high tolerance of contradictions." Later, he expands on this theme, noting, "It can be a frustrating phenomenon for a pastor to minister to parishioners who affirm the authority of the Bible and are active members of conservative churches, but who hold liberal views on cohabitation, divorce and remarriage, materialism, drugs, and alcohol. Even if the Boomer does not personally live with seeming contradiction he or she may be much more tolerant than his or her parents toward the differing views of others."[7]

Ministering to Boomer Believers

"Traditional Christian denominations will have their chance for growth and resurgence . . . ," writes James Scudder of the Gannett News Service. "But only if they become less stodgy and bend to meet the real personal needs of people who come to them."[8]

Church attendance among Boomers, particularly older ones, rose in the late 1980s and early 1990s. At 42 percent of those born between 1946 and 1958, the rate was close to the percentage of their counterparts during the Depression era.[9] Middle-aged Boomers seem to be returning to many of our country's traditional values. Many LEBs have made their way back to churches. This will probably also be true of TREBs as they progress through middle age.[10] Although many

Boomers are looking for spiritual renewal in their lives, they are not always returning to the denominations they attended as children. A study reported in *Progressions*, a Lilly Endowment Occasional Report, summarizes what is happening among returning Boomers.

> In general, the Boomers are seen as "consumers" looking to get something specific from a church, should they choose to join one. They are fussier (or more discriminating) than were their parents and will shop around to find the preacher, the spiritual atmosphere or the church school believed to fulfill their needs. They are—by general agreement of those who study them—not only picky, but highly pragmatic. Those who go back to church look for two things in particular: religious education for their children and some kind of religious experience that helps them make sense of their own lives.[11]

The following are some specific ways a church can attract and keep the Boomer generation.

Highlight Purpose and Vision

Boomers often find churches dull and lacking excitement. They are attracted to a church that has a clearly stated purpose supported by specific plans. Remember, Boomers belong to a generation that fights for causes. They have led antiwar, human rights, and world hunger efforts. They need to know that a church has a vision of what God wants it to be and do.

John F. Kennedy left a legacy of activism to Boomers that caused them to focus on changing their world. As they have matured, they have turned their activist interest toward local issues. Churches that can cast a vision of ministry in areas close to home will be able to capture the interest and commitment of the Boomer.

Plan Celebrative Worship Services

Churches that perpetuate a traditional model of worship may find it difficult to keep Boomers. Those who leave traditional churches are often attracted to churches that have celebrative and participative worship services with contemporary music. Many Boomers find celebrative services meaningful because they are involved in the worship experience.

Celebrative services usually emphasize great themes of the faith, praise and worship, and congregational participation. They are fast paced, well planned, and rehearsed, with small bands often providing the accompaniment for the praise songs.

Having become used to the short, entertaining bursts of information provided by television, Boomers may not respond to the traditional sermon format. Consider the following.

- Stress practical application, not just content, in preaching and Bible teaching.
- Make sermons no longer than thirty minutes.
- Use a variety of teaching methods. Experiment with drama productions and video to illustrate the truths of Scripture.

Stress Quality

Boomers have higher expectations than their Builder parents for quality in programming, facilities, and music in their churches. Lyle Schaller observes, "A new generation of people have come on the scene who expect attractive nurseries, air-conditioning, excellent acoustics, convenient off-street parking, carpeted rooms, comfortable chairs, attractive rest rooms, and many other amenities of life that were considered luxuries in the earlier years of the 20th century."[12]

Boomers understand that a church is not a business, but they want it to be businesslike in terms of quality and efficiency. They expect good business practices in the handling of finances and long-range planning and understand how computers, fax machines, and cellular phones can aid a church's ministry.

Streamline Structure

The typical week for an average Boomer has very little uncommitted time. Two-thirds of Boomer wives work outside the home, compared to about 57 percent in the rest of the female population. Work that was often done during the day thirty years ago—for example, grocery shopping and house-cleaning—now must be done on the "second shift" after working partners come home. Two-income partners scramble to catch up with chores at night and on weekends. Though they may want to be involved in the church, they do not have large blocks of time that they can commit.

To encourage Boomer participation, churches must stream-line their structure, eliminating needless positions, committees, and boards. They should also evaluate programs and use only those proven to be successful, clustering several events together so people can have fewer nights out. For training, churches can use weekend retreats and short seminars that do not require long-term attendance. Schedules should be made with commuters, working women, and dual-earner households in mind.

Recruit people for service based on their gifts rather than the church's need, and recruit for shorter periods of commitment. Boomers have found that it works well to delegate decisions to small groups of concerned people who have the authority and responsibility to act. Boomers are more apt to be involved in programs if they have participated in the decision making.

Offer Multiple Options

It was a 31-Flavors-Baskin-Robbins world that Boomers grew up in, and they continue to enjoy nearly unlimited choice in everything from food to entertainment. Shopping centers with hundreds of stores under one roof and acres of parking are now the norm. Superstores offering clothing, groceries, and hardware are becoming popular. Restaurants with a variety of cuisines line every city's main streets. And entertainment is cheap and varied through videos, DVDs, cable TV, and the Internet.

It is not surprising, then, that Boomers are attracted to churches that offer a variety of programs, ministries, and services. They expect ministries geared to various age groups, small-group Bible studies, and preschools.

Smaller churches can attract Boomers by concentrating on the ministries and programs they do best, making sure they are high quality. They should establish one or two specialized ministries and then gradually add new ministries when the resources needed for quality ministry are available.

Use Small Groups

Place a healthy emphasis on relationships through the development of small-group ministries. Boomers tend to like small groups because of their interest in the personal application of teaching and in relationships. This could mean that Boomers would choose to do Bible study in groups that do not meet on Sunday morning and are not content-oriented, as traditional adult Sunday school classes are. Groups that discuss issues, minister to personal needs, and offer close relationships often appeal to Boomers.

Restructure Existing Services

Some services in traditional churches could be restructured so that they would be more attractive to Boomers. For example, churches have traditionally held two worship services on Sunday, one in the morning and one in the evening. The morning service uses the varsity team. The congregation will hear the best musicians, the best sermons, and the best drama. The second string is brought in for Sunday evening. For this service, the pastor's sermon is not as well prepared, and the musicians are often people who need a little more practice before playing in the morning service. The entire evening service seems to drop down a notch or two in terms of quality.

Boomers, who are time and quality conscious, usually do not support such a service. Some churches have restructured the evening service by building in time for families, sponsoring a Bible institute in the same time slot, organizing small groups to meet in homes, and even moving adult education to Sunday evenings. In the last decade, some have started experimenting with worship services on Friday and Saturday evenings with good success.

Communicate Visually

Boomers are a visual generation. Raised on TV, Boomers like to see as well as hear the message of the gospel. A trend that began to develop in the late '60s and has blossomed over the years is the projection of worship songs on a screen. When people look up at a screen, they raise their heads and sing out louder.

A natural extension of the projection of songs in a worship service is the use of video. It is a rare church that does not have video equipment for use in the children's or youth department. Adult small groups often use Christian videos for teaching or Bible study. Found in numerous churches, but not in large use yet, is video and computer projection in the main worship services of the church. Some churches have started using video and computer projection as a means of giving announcements during worship services and as a creative way to illustrate the pastor's message.

Related to all this is the use of small dramas during worship. These short (about five-minute) dramas draw people into the theme of the worship service in very powerful and personal ways. They fit the Boomer generation well since they offer a visual experience of the message.

Expand the Roles of Women

Women are greatly influencing our society. The number of companies in the United States owned or controlled by women has grown to the point where they now employ more people than do all the Fortune 500 companies. Churches are wise not to waste this valuable resource. Take seriously the gifts, talents, calling, and proven ability of women. Create new ministries that will challenge and use the gifts of your women members. Schedule church services and meetings to fit working women's time constraints. Develop courses and seminars that will speak to the needs of women. Show your women members that you take them seriously by hiring a director of women's ministry.

Focus on Local Ministries

LEBs spent a great deal of their lives trying to change society. They focused on the big issues of life such as civil rights and world peace. Looking back, they question whether much was accomplished, and in frustration, many prefer to focus their ministry efforts in local arenas, where they feel they have more control and can see the results of their work.

Churches can take advantage of this by developing and emphasizing ministries that are "over here" rather than "over there." Churches can focus on the needs in their immediate neighborhood and the concerns important to their community and then organize efforts to meet some of these concerns.

Offer Short-Term Missions Involvement

Boomers, of course, can also develop interest in overseas missions, especially if they become personally involved. James F. Engel, writing in *Christianity Today*, declares, "If international vision is to be expanded, direct exposure and involvement overseas is an absolute necessity; short-term service is the key to the problem." He goes on to say, "Our data from the Wheaton Graduate School study clearly demonstrate that those who have been involved overseas, even for a brief visit, have significantly greater awareness of the commitment to world evangelization."[13] Boomers may not give a lifetime to missions, but they may be willing to serve for a short time.

Conclusion

Churches that minister effectively to Boomers take seriously Boomer values, needs, and concerns. For example, since Boomers are experience-oriented, churches will take pains to provide ways for Boomers to experience Christianity. Since Boomers are future-oriented, churches must focus on tomorrow more than yesterday. Since Boomers are growth-oriented, a church must look beyond current membership to those who do not yet believe. Since Boomers are people-oriented, churches must be less concerned with programs and more concerned with the needs of people. And since Boomers are action-oriented, churches must do rather than just discuss.

In *Baby Boom Believers,* author Mike Bellah warns us that "the baby boom is simply too big and too influential to be ignored. Industries have been made or broken by the baby boom. Businesses have learned the hard way that you neglect the baby boom at your own peril."[14] Churches that want to grow must not ignore the Boomer generation but adjust their ministries to attract and keep them.

Reaching the Boomer Generation

6

A Texas-based group—the American Association of Boomers (AAB)—was organized in June 1989 to channel the clout of seventy-six million Boomers. Modeled after the American Association for Retired Persons (AARP), AAB's goal is to advance the social, professional, and economic status of Boomers. *My Generation,* AAB's newsletter, covers political, financial, and social issues such as health care. Articles have included "The AARP Is Picking Our Pockets" and "Boomers in the Electronic Age—Tapping Our Electronic Power."

Other newsletters have been launched in an attempt to harness the tremendous power of Boomers. *Boomerang* was started by editor Jo-Ann Fitzgerald Conroy to provide information of interest to this generation and a forum for discussing issues, such as the environment, economy, family, job changes, and the stress of dual-income marriages. Cheryl Russell edits *The Boomer Report,* providing insights to reach America's most influential group.

Boomers are now wielding a huge amount of political clout. In past years, when Boomers were preoccupied with their professions and personal lives, Builders had a disproportionate influence in local elections. Boomers have been cynical about politics, and this too has kept them from voting. In 1989, however, Boomer voters began to control the outcomes of many local elections across the United States. Writing about Boomer influence on the Seattle city elections in 1989, Walter Hatch notes that "younger voters torpedoed all of those candidates. . . . This may be the first time that younger voters have controlled the outcome of a local election."[1]

Today more than half of all households are headed by persons born between 1946 and 1964. These midlife Boomers are more open to spiritual things. Sadly their spiritual needs are often being met by the New Age movement rather than by the Christian church. There are indications that unchurched Baby Boomers are open to the gospel. How can we effectively reach them in the coming years?

Growing Spiritual Openness

Writing in 1985 sociologist Charles Schewe of the University of Massachusetts stated, "I don't expect yuppies to live forever as yuppies. As they age, have families and take on new responsibilities there will be a new lifestyle, a new look and a new value system for them."[2] Now we see the reality of his predictions.

The oldest Boomers will turn fifty-six in 2002, a strange thought for a generation that once declared they would not trust anyone over thirty. This is forcing them to come face-to-face with the second half century of their lives. Menopause looms in the immediate future for many Boomer women. Boomer men are balding. Wrinkles and heartburn cannot be far away. The new three Rs for Boomers are Reeboks, Rogaine, and Retin-A. Their new battle cry may be "Gray is good."

A survey of 1,600 Boomers concerning their church attendance found that about 33 percent can be labeled loyalists, never having left organized religion. Twenty-five percent can be labeled returnees, those who have come back to church. But the largest group, 42 percent, left church and have still not returned, although they have spiritual leanings. Further, Boomers can be divided into "mystics" and "theists." The mystics see God within themselves and are attracted by New Age teachings. The theists see an eternal source of spiritual authority, though not necessarily the God of the Bible.[3] Leading-Edge Boomers, who grew up in the counterculture of the 1960s, tend to be the ones who believe all religions are equally good. It is the Trailing-Edge Boomers—who actually attend church less—that are the more religious in the traditional sense.[4] Here are some indications that Boomers are slowing down for God.

Traditional Values

A national telephone survey of one thousand Boomers by the American Council of Life Insurance found that Boomers want stronger family and religious ties. They desire a greater respect for authority and stricter moral values. Concerns about morals and religious training for their children appear to be a major reason for Boomers' returning to church. These concerns are not the only reasons, however. Many Boomers are asking very deep questions about their lives. For nearly three decades Boomers did not take seriously the institution of marriage. It was free love in the 1960s, finding oneself in the 1970s, and searching for success in the 1980s. In the 1990s many Boomers headed back to the traditional home. "We'll see that relationships can't be taken for granted anymore," says Dr. Samuel Pauker, one of more than fifty experts surveyed by *Bride's* magazine.[5]

The twenty-first century will be a more grown-up era for Boomers. The reason? They are moving through middle age. The values they had in the '60s no longer satisfy as they have matured. Ann Clurman, vice president of Grey Advertising, expands on the Boomer search for values. "There is a free-floating sense of searching for a value system. All the instincts of the baby Boomers are saying, 'Slow down. Figure out what's important.' But they haven't arrived at what that is."[6]

Loss of a Fantasy

Since 1983 when the term *Yuppie* first appeared in print, more than twenty-two thousand articles have been written on the subject. In reality very few Boomers fit the profile of a Yuppie. Only about 5 percent of the Boomer population made the grade of age (young), income (high), geography (urban), attitude (selfish), and affections (BMWs).

But, of course, almost all had the fantasy—built on the concept of generational entitlement rooted in the prosperity of the '50s and '60s. The idea of having it all appealed to almost the entire generation. In a sense, yuppiedom was the natural outgrowth of the hedonism of the 1960s and the obsessive meism of the 1970s. Its materialism filled a void left by the neglect of God and traditional values.

By 1986 some declared that the Yuppie was dead. The death was brought about by family, finances, and fatigue. The wanton consumption—the getting-and-spending frenzy of the early 1980s—came to a halt with the arrival of the recession. Gone for most are the Mercedes and his-and-her Rolexes. With corporate cutbacks, businesses have said good-bye to middle managers, and many Boomers have had to tone down their materialistic lifestyles. The lavish upscalers of the '80s are now the frugal downscalers of the early twenty-first century. BMWs are traded for Fords (well, at least Hondas), and credit cards are cut up. The instincts of the Boomer today say, "Slow down and find out what's important."

Slower Lifestyle

Commuter marriages and job transfers causing uprooting of families are by-products of a high-pressure, success-oriented lifestyle. This was exciting when Boomers were younger but has taken its toll on couples who have not had the time and energy to cement their marriages and families together. Deep down Boomers are hurting. Wade Clark Roof says, "We are all leading lives of quiet desperation. There is definitely a reclaiming of spirituality among many Boomers involved in what is at least in part a midlife quest for meaning."[7]

An article in *USA Today,* titled "Baby Boomers Hit Brakes after Life in the Fast Lane," details how the changing marriage and growing family are slowing down Baby Boomers to a more reasonable pace of life. Those Boomers who can afford it and are willing to take the career risk are moving to communities with less stress, crime, smog, and people. They want a nice quiet place to live and think seriously about their spiritual lives.[8]

Dr. Melvyn Kinder suggests in his book *Going Nowhere Fast* that Boomers want to get off seven different treadmills:

- ambition treadmill
- money treadmill
- personal appearance treadmill
- sexual performance treadmill
- waiting-for-love treadmill
- marriage/divorce treadmill
- raising-perfect-children treadmill[9]

Job Competition and Finances

July 20, 1988, was a significant date to demographers. On that date the group of those aged thirty-five to fifty-nine equaled and began to exceed the size of the eighteen to thirty-four-year-old group. As Boomers continue to move through middle age, this older portion of the population will become its fastest growing segment. Right now the number of young workers is declining and the number of prime-age employees is exploding. In effect, everyone who will be working in the first decade of the 2000s has already been born, and two-thirds of them are at work today.[10]

As businesses downsize, old jobs are eliminated and new jobs open up, often forcing middle-aged Boomers back into the job market. Younger Busters are advancing up the promotion ladder, and since older workers expect more in terms of benefits and compensation, employers are often willing to replace them with younger and less costly workers, even Bridgers just entering the job market.

Burdened with mortgages and family costs, prime-age Boomers face stresses they never encountered before. The American Dream traditionally included finding a good job, purchasing a home, and raising a happy family. Sometimes included in the dream were Mom at home full-time, a large yard with a dog, and piano lessons and good schools for the kids.

Money magazine reports a study by Lawrence Eisenstein, a New Jersey psychiatrist, who asked thirteen hundred middle-aged people to name their greatest concern. Seventy percent replied "having enough money to cover expenses." Common fears were having to support aging parents, getting divorced or outliving their spouse, supporting stepchildren, and paying for children's college education. Many Boomers "have merely been treading water," writes Frank Levy of the University of Maryland. They are barely making it financially.

A high-spending group, Boomers are just beginning to think about retirement. With little trust in Social Security, many are starting to worry about having enough for a comfortable retirement. Most analysts project that the Social Security program is sound until around 2030, but after that no one is quite sure what will happen. In 2030 most Boomers will have retired, some just beginning to draw Social Security. Boomers wonder how long there will be money to draw. Add to this the drop in stock values following the terrorist attack on New York City and the Pentagon on September 11, 2001, and Boomers are shifting focus from early retirement to long-term investing.

Reevaluating Goals

The corporate battle that was exhilarating to the thirty-year-old manager often seems empty and futile to the midlife executive. More than 60 percent of career people are "working wounded." The Vietnam War forced many young men to move into college and careers because they wanted to avoid being drafted. Many made career choices that have not been satisfying. Women wonder if working outside the home is worth the personal sacrifices they have had to make. As a result, many Boomers are heading back to school and starting second careers, all the while reevaluating their work, family, and personal development. Midlife Boomers often realize that jobs have taken them far away from old friends and family members. Thus they are redefining *family*. Family to many Boomers is any group of people whose members love and care for each other.

As Boomers grow through middle age, they are realizing that the materialistic "me" approach is not satisfying. They are beginning to work together. Their top concerns for the twenty-first century are ethics, environmentalism, and meaningful experiences, all of which can best be accomplished together. Out with the "me" generation, in with the "we" generation is the new view. Now there is discussion of the value of self-fulfillment versus responsibility, individual ambition versus the needs of others, living together versus marriage, and liberal social values versus conservative social values.

Maturity

Boomers have grown up. A reflection of the Boomer maturation is evident in the new music being sung by rock stars who grew up with the Boomers, like Bruce Springsteen, James Taylor, and Eric Clapton. These headliners are still doing tours, but today Springsteen, 49, sings about fatherhood, Taylor, 51, about the devastated environment, and Clapton, 54, about the death of his son.

Marketers are beginning to target an aging Boomer generation with new products designed specifically for them. Maybelline, for example, is in hot pursuit of aging Boomers. With an eight-million-dollar advertising budget, Maybelline launched a new line of makeup for women aged thirty-five and older. Using "age-appropriate" models, they sell their new age-defying makeup, called Maybelline Revitalizing.

Reaching Unchurched Boomers

As Boomers have moved through the normal stages of life, they have come to realize that there is no salvation in secular society. Now as many of them move through midlife, part of their midlife crisis is an intensifying search for meaning.

Faith is coming to bear on the lives of Boomers, but they still shy away from organized religion. At the heart of their search for faith, notes sociologist Wade Clark Roof, is a deep yearning for "meaning and belonging. There is a kind of spiritual renewal occurring among members of this generation," writes Roof, "but it does not necessarily mean a return to organized religion."[11]

A generation ago religion was considered to be a very private matter. Today many choose lifestyles closely aligned with religious beliefs. Jimmy Carter, Charles Colson, and other high-profile individuals serve as models. Churches can effectively reach Boomers as they strategically target their outreach ministries to meet Boomer needs and interests.

Emphasize Family

As Boomers have aged, they have become more intensely involved with their children. Since 1992 several new magazines have been launched that highlight growing family needs and interests. Jann S. Wenner, who founded *Rolling Stone* over a quarter century ago and became a leading voice of the Boomer generation, premiered *Family Life* in 1993. It is aimed at parents in their thirties and forties with children under twelve years old.

Wenner was not the first to recognize the new Boomer interest in families or to start a magazine aimed at them. Several years ago, Jake Winebaum started *Family Fun* magazine, which he sold to the Walt Disney Company in 1992.

These magazines deal with topics that are now of interest to Boomers, but they cannot meet the deep needs of Boomers. In fact no other institution has the resources that churches do to help Boomer families. Marriage and family ministries have long been the foundational ministries for many churches. Churches have the knowledge and resources to lead searching Boomers into lifelong commitments, healthy child rearing, and strong family units. But churches must take their knowledge into the marketplace by offering seminars and workshops on parenting in the community. Unchurched Boomers are not likely to walk into a Sunday school class on parenting.

Develop Bridge Ministries

There is a need for "bridge ministries" to help unchurched Boomers move into a church. Focusing on building relationships with unchurched people in the community, bridge ministries encourage people to become familiar with the church before they are ready to be a part of it. Effective bridge ministries include:

- Offering career guidance. Many Boomers are changing careers and may need help identifying their abilities, their goals, and their passions. Other Boomers lost jobs when the technology market suffered a collapse in 2000 and 2001. Courses in career planning will help Boomers retool for the future.
- Small groups for stepparents. A high divorce rate and an equally high remarriage rate have led to a dramatic increase in the number of stepfamilies in our communities. The Stepfamily Association of America estimates that thirteen hundred new stepfamilies are being formed every day in the United States. There are some thirty-five million stepparents. A study reported by the Stepfamily Association of America reported that 30 percent of all children under eighteen years old are living in a stepfamily.[12]
- Other helpful ministries are a divorce-care workshop, an out-of-work support group, and a parents-of-AIDS-victims support group. A singles ministry; support groups for those combating drug addiction, alcoholism, or homosexuality; marital counseling and marriage enrichment seminars are

other types of ministries that could serve as bridges to the unchurched Boomer.

Develop a Seeker Service

A large number of churches have found that the addition of a second worship service targeted directly to Boomers is a successful way to reach them with the gospel. A seeker service should

- use contemporary music
- stress praise and worship
- allow participation, such as clapping
- use audiovisual media
- use Scripture from a modern translation
- print first-class bulletins
- encourage conversation before and after the service
- limit preaching to twenty to thirty minutes
- stress practical living
- provide alternate ways to acknowledge acceptance of Christ, such as with decision cards

It is important to make guests feel welcome. Enter the door of a Wal-Mart store, and you will be greeted by a friendly person who offers you a shopping cart. Wal-Mart understands the need to greet guests graciously, and their success has prompted competitors such as Target and K-Mart to follow suit.

To welcome Boomer guests, be sure to

- give them the best parking
- give them the best seats
- hold worship services at convenient times
- provide a visitors center
- use trained greeters

- offer a welcome packet of valuable information
- make good use of directional signs
- provide a fellowship time after worship that makes guests feel welcome
- welcome them from the pulpit but do not have them stand and speak

Stress Lifestyle Evangelism

Train members to develop friendships with the unchurched and give them time to do it by limiting the number of church activities. Organize nonthreatening events, such as parties and concerts to which the unchurched can be invited. Valentine banquets, harvest dinners, and Sunday school picnics can all be planned to help make the unchurched feel comfortable.

Members should invite friends to worship services. Lyle Schaller describes congregations that effectively invite Boomers to church:

> The congregations in which members invite others to come to church with them usually display these characteristics: a) members are enthusiastic about their faith, b) members are enthusiastic about their congregation, c) members are enthusiastic about the current pastor, d) the congregation, as a whole, conveys the expectation that members will invite others, e) most members actively and enthusiastically greet and welcome visitors, f) the worship experience is planned with the assumption that first-time visitors will be present.[13]

Build on the desire for relationships by developing small groups. Use a combination of Bible studies, fellowship groups, social groups, task groups, accountability groups, and support groups. Don't forget the draw of sports for both men and women. Boomer women enjoy fitness, and many of them will be attracted to coed volleyball teams, aerobics classes, and jogging groups. Reliance on one type of group, such as Bible studies, will usually not work. Give Boomers multiple choices.

Offer Opportunities for Service

"We are the generation that makes a difference" declares the headline on a brochure from the American Association of Boomers. Inside it begins, "When we were younger, we wanted to make a difference." Boomers have long had a desire to serve others. Think of ways you might be able to involve unchurched Boomers in your church ministries. Of course, there are places of service that are inappropriate for an unchurched person to serve, such as a Sunday school teacher or board member, but there may be places where they can serve and build a relationship with your church, which could lead to their hearing and receiving the gospel. Be sure to

- recruit through personal contact
- ask for short commitments
- emphasize team ministry and play down superstar ministry
- provide training

Get Involved in the Community

Many, if not most, of today's churches focus the bulk of their energy internally on the people who are already there. Activist Boomers are attracted to organizations, especially churches, that take their message to the streets. Churches that hope to reach Boomers for Christ must get their hands dirty in ministry in their local communities. Begin by asking questions of civic leaders and reading local newspapers and then make a list of the needs and concerns in your immediate community. Share the findings with your people. Ask people to pray about these needs and expect God to place burdens on people about becoming involved in finding answers. Look for four or five people who are interested in helping others solve their problems. Organize them into a task force and give them training and perhaps a little start-up capital but expect them to carry the weight and burden of making the ministry go.

Minister to Singles

According to *U.S. News and World Report,* fewer than 3 percent of the population lived alone in 1940. By 1995 that number had risen to nearly 12 percent of the population. More than 50 percent of those living alone are women. While many singles are widows or widowers, there are increasing numbers of people who have chosen not to marry. And the number of singles who have been divorced will increase as people continue to follow the script of *Kramer vs. Kramer* rather than *Ozzie and Harriet.* The number of Americans who had never been married reached 8.3 percent in 1994, the highest recorded number in twenty-five years.[14]

Create multiple options in singles ministry. Typical college and career groups will flourish, but groups targeted to midlife-never-married singles will enable your church to stand apart from others. Design social activities for parents without partners. Create classes that deal with the single lifestyle. Establish divorce-care programs. Create a church atmosphere of acceptance for singles. Rethink the concept of a "family" church.

Use Sports and Retreats

When most of us think of camps we think of kids, hot dogs, ghost stories, name tags, sleeping bags, and bunks. But camp is no longer exclusively for kids. New camps specifically designed for adults are springing up everywhere, and old ones are retooling to meet the demands of adult audiences. For example, one- and two-week camps costing one thousand dollars or more offer training from tennis to golf to mountain climbing to sailing. Instead of hot dogs, there are low-fat, high-energy diets for active people. In place of counselors, there are coaches and trainers. Along with fun, there is the desire to improve old skills and learn new ones. Many offer up to six hours each day of training and discussion on fitness and diet.

A different slant to this is the living out of fantasies through camps such as fantasy baseball camps where retired baseball players coach and play games with those who remember them.

Then there are the members of the Cowboy Lawyers Association in Los Angeles who annually go to Colorado to live and work a few days on a western dude ranch. These "city slickers" live out their fantasies and reduce their stress all at the same time. Boomers, who are often nostalgic about old movies, television shows, and sports heroes, enjoy these camps.

Churches can take advantage of the Boomer interest in sports activities by organizing hiking; softball, basketball, and volleyball teams; as well as aerobics classes and other similar activities. Host a doubles tennis tournament where members invite nonmembers to play with them. Or have your own sports camps. In addition, adult retreats can be sponsored with themes such as Building Strong Relationships or Living Healthy and Happy.

Plant a Daughter Church

At least 100,000 new churches are needed in the United States to reach the Boomer generation (as well as the younger Busters and Bridgers). New churches often bring a new style of ministry that is attractive to these middle-aged adults. They allow for the creation of new structures, are more open to new people, and create more vision and challenge than older churches. Planting a daughter church also brings new life and vitality to the mother church as vision and excitement are enhanced with the birth of the new congregation.

Conclusion

A decade ago Elmer Towns encouraged churches to retool to reach the Boomer generation. His words still need to be taken seriously. "We must understand them now to reach them before it is too late. The coming Boomer Church can influence our culture but the congregations that ignore them will only be hibernating churches."[15]

The Boomer generation has had tremendous impact on our society. The size of this generation has caused overcrowded classrooms and an overcrowded job market. As Boomers continue to mature and their desires and tastes change, their needs will not be met as they were in the past, and their needs are very different from those of Builders when they were in midlife.

To effectively reach Boomers with the gospel, we need to correct our tunnel vision that has never allowed us to change our method of sharing the gospel. With a desire to reach Boomers and a willingness to tailor ministry to them, we can bring many to Christ in the years to come.

The Boomer Generation

Aliases	Yuppies (young, urban professionals)
	Oinks (one income, no kids)
	Dinks (double income, no kids)
	New Collars (information workers)
	Gold Collars (highly paid information workers)
	Postwar Babies
	Postwar generation
	Vietnam generation
	Sixties generation
	Challengers
	Me generation
Formative Years	1950s, 1960s, and 1970s
Formative Experiences	Cold War
	Television
	Economic affluence
	Education and technology
	Rock and roll
	Civil Rights movement
	The new frontier
	Space race
	Assassinations
	Vietnam War and Kent State
	Energy crisis
	Watergate and Nixon resignation
Characteristics	Educated
	Media-oriented
	Independent
	Cause-oriented
	Fitness conscious
	Rock music fans
	Activists
	Quality conscious
	Questioners of authority
Religious Characteristics	Committed to relationships
	Want to belong
	Supportive of people
	Want to live their faith
	Want experiences with faith
	Tolerant of differences

Boomer Ministry

Highlight purpose and vision
Use celebrative worship
Stress quality
Streamline structure
Offer multiple options
Use small groups
Restructure existing services
Communicate visually
Expand roles of women
Focus on local ministry
Offer short-term missions involvement

Common Needs and Concerns

Spiritual search
Desire to return to traditional values
Slower lifestyle
Second career development
Financial worries
Reevaluating goals
Midlife transitions
Preparing for retirement
Death of the American Dream

Reaching Unchurched Boomers

Emphasize family
Develop bridge ministries
Develop a seeker service
Stress lifestyle evangelism
Offer opportunities for service
Get involved in the community
Welcome guests appropriately
Create opportunities for belonging
Minister to singles
Use sports and retreats
Plant a daughter church

Part 3

The Buster
Wave

Why Are They Called Busters?

7

The *Simpsons* television show is not known for saving people's lives. But in 1992 an episode was credited with helping to save the life of an eight-year-old boy. Karen Bencze of Auburn, Washington, informed Fox executives (producers of the sitcom) that her eight-year-old son was choking on a piece of orange when his ten-year-old brother performed the Heimlich maneuver on him, a technique he learned from a February episode of *The Simpsons*. After learning of the story, an executive producer of the series commented "It's great. Everyone at *The Simpsons* was shocked that anyone learned anything from our show. We'll try not to ever let that happen again."[1]

For some people *The Simpsons* pictures the Buster generation perfectly. To them, it is a wonder that the MTV generation learned anything. But such a limited concept of the Buster generation is unfair. Like the Builders and Boomers before them, Busters are a complex mix that cannot be generalized too narrowly.

Broadly defined, Busters were born between 1965 and 1983 and represent sixty-six million Americans. They are called Busters because theirs is a smaller (bust) generation compared to their Boomer parents who make up the largest single generation in our history—seventy-seven million. Of course, sixty-six million Busters is not such a small number. It is the third largest generation to be born in the United States (following the Boomers and Bridgers) and honestly is not much of a bust. The term bust was actually given to only the first twelve years of the generation (1965–1976) when only forty-one million babies were born. Compared to the seventy-seven million Boomers, this was a bust. Over the years the name has been used to include the entire generation. Total births in the Buster generation were 65,808,000 (24 percent of the population) but immigration has swelled their ranks to nearly seventy-six million or 27 percent of the U.S. population as of 2002.

Buster Births

1965	3,760,000	1972	3,258,000	1979	3,473,000
1966	3,606,000	1973	3,137,000	1980	3,612,000
1967	3,521,000	1974	3,160,000	1981	3,629,000
1968	3,502,000	1975	3,144,000	1982	3,681,000
1969	3,571,000	1976	3,168,000	1983	3,639,000
1970	3,731,000	1977	3,327,000		
1971	3,556,000	1978	3,333,000		

Like their predecessors, Busters have been given numerous aliases in an attempt to characterize their distinctives. *Time* called them the Twentysomething Generation. *Fortune* has referred to them as Yiffies, for young, individualistic, freedom-minded, and few. *Esquire* has labeled them the Nowhere Generation. Names such as Post-Boomers (Posties), Echo Boom, and Baby Boomlet link them directly to their Boomer parents' generation. Twentysomethings and Thirtysomethings point to their primary age. The 13ers name recognizes them as the thirteenth generation since America's founding fathers. Generation X, a name taken from the title of Douglas Coupland's 1991 novel, has been the most popular. However, it is not well liked by members of this generation. With its many negative connotations, the term is being used less and less.

Busters, of course, are the children of the Boomers. Born between 1965 and 1983, they are now between the ages of nineteen and thirty-seven. Like the generations before them, Busters are not a homogeneous whole but may be divided into two distinct groups: the Bust and the Boomlet.

The Bust

Born between 1965 and 1976, Baby Busters are those between the ages of twenty-six and thirty-seven and represent forty-one million people (49.6 million with immigration). Most of the studies of Busters have been made on this cohort.

Influential Members of the Baby Bust

Troy Aikman, 36	LL Cool J, 34	Adam Sandler, 35
Lisa Bonet, 35	Greg Maddux, 36	Brooke Shields, 37
Johnny Depp, 39	Shaquille O'Neal, 29	Todd Stottlemyre, 37
Leonardo DiCaprio, 28	Mary Lou Retton, 34	Malcolm Jamal
Steffi Graf, 33	Julia Roberts, 34	Warner, 32
Ken Griffey Jr., 33	Winona Ryder, 31	
Janet Jackson, 36	Gabriela Sabatini, 32	

Ages as of 2002

The Boomlet

Many Boomers married later in life or, if they got married at a young age, did not have children until their careers were established. The result has been a Baby Boomlet (sometimes referred to as an Echo Boom). This second phase of births comprises the last seven years of the Buster generation (1977–1983). Total head count of Boomlet babies is roughly twenty-five million (26.8 million with immigration). They are nineteen to twenty-five years old today. Although the term *Generation X* has been used to include the entire Buster generation, it specifically represents this younger Boomlet.

Influential Members of the Baby Boomlet		
Macaulay Culkin, 22	Joey Lawrence, 24	Jodie Sweetin, 20
Eddie Furlong, 25	Fred Savage, 24	Elijah Wood, 21
Balthazar Getty, 25	Britney Spears, 19	

Ages as of 2002

Researchers seeking to characterize the Buster generation have often made two mistakes. First, they think this generation is extremely cynical. Second, they believe it is only a younger version of the Boomers. Both, of course, are not correct. Busters have had a bad rap. Calling them Generation X and portraying all of them as a whining group of cynical youth is as inaccurate as calling all Boomers hippies. Likewise, assuming Busters are small versions of the Boomers misses the nuances that make them different from their Boomer parents. Like all generations, they have experienced similar events that have shaped a general character, and this allows us to see them as a distinct group.

The development of the Busters as a generation is important to our nation, for by the year 2015, Busters will begin to take over leadership of the United States. It will take that long for two reasons: The Boomer generation is blocking their way, and a generation normally does not take over until a majority of its members enter their forties.

Shaping the Busters

Enough time has gone by for the Buster generation to see some prime events, inventions, and experiences that have affected their thinking and living.

Roe v. Wade

Roe v. Wade was a decision by the United States Supreme Court in 1973 concerning a woman's right to an abortion. The

Court determined that a state could not restrict abortion during the first three months of pregnancy but could regulate abortions during the second trimester to protect a woman's health. During the final trimester states are allowed to prohibit abortions unless the pregnancy endangers the woman's health. One of the most controversial Supreme Court decisions of all time, it has been challenged and modified but remains in place.

Since the oldest Buster was only eight years old at the time of *Roe v. Wade*, none of them will remember it directly. It has been a life-shaping event for their generation, however, since it has limited their birth rate dramatically. There is little doubt that the Buster generation might have outstripped the Boomer generation in size if babies had been born rather than aborted.[2]

High Technology

Growth of technology has skyrocketed during the Buster years. As an example, between 1946 and 1960 the number of computers grew from one to ten thousand. From 1960 to 1980 the number grew to ten million. By the year 2000 there were more than eighty million computers in the United States alone. The number of components that can be programmed into a computer chip doubled every eighteen months during that period of time.[3] Today it is a rare business, church, and even home that is without a computer. Busters are very comfortable with computers. In contrast, the Builder generation grew up writing by hand and using manual typewriters. Boomers started with manual typewriters and moved up to electric models. The youngest of the Busters have never used a typewriter but usually are computer literate.

Video Games and Television

The popularity of video games is enormous. Atari founder Nathan Bushnell introduced the first video game in 1972. Pong, a simple tennis game, sold more than six thousand units its first year. In 1989 Nintendo's Super Mario Brothers 3 sold more than seven million units in the first year. More recently their

Mortal Kombat game sold nearly four million in its first six months of release. The video game market grew so rapidly during the 1980s that in 1992 a search was made to determine the largest installed base of chip-driven devices in U.S. homes. Surprisingly it was not found to be IBM or Macintosh computers or even chip-driven appliances but 48.8 million Nintendos! The rapid-fire image changes in almost all video games mean that Busters who play them have had to develop visual acuity and the ability to respond quickly.

In the past two decades there has been a tremendous change in what is available to watch on television. With hundreds of cable stations to choose from, viewers have endless variety. There are fewer restrictions on program content today than just a few years ago, and violence and immorality are continuous fare. MTV, a network that appeals to young people through its often explicit music videos and its counterculture programming, was estimated to reach twenty million twelve to twenty five year olds in 1995.

Our technology today has made it possible for events to be televised as they happen. This has meant that people can watch crises anywhere in the world as they develop. A moment-by-moment account of Desert Storm, the assassination attempt on Ronald Reagan in 1981, or O. J. Simpson's slow drive on the Los Angeles freeway before giving himself up to the police certainly have had an impact on Buster viewers. In 1979, when Iran took American hostages and held them for 441 days, television viewers saw images of the hooded victims over and over and were reminded nightly of the crisis. This detailed coverage of current events as they happen may make it difficult for Busters to separate fact from fiction, because they appear almost like a video game.

The Challenger Disaster

On January 28, 1986, the space shuttle *Challenger* exploded moments after lifting off at Cape Canaveral, Florida. All crew members were killed, including the first private citizen astronaut, New Hampshire schoolteacher Christa McAuliffe. A later investigation discovered that a seal on a solid-fuel booster rocket was the prime cause of the explosion. The tragedy shook NASA and the world as the explosion took place on national television. The horrendous images on television shook up many Busters, who were between the ages of three and twenty-one at the time. The *Challenger* disaster had an effect on older Busters that was similar to the impact that the assassinations of JFK and Dr. King had on their Boomer parents and that the attack on Pearl Harbor had on their Builder grandparents.

Berlin Wall Dismantled

East Germany built the Berlin Wall in 1961 as a barrier to stop the exodus of refugees from Communist East Germany to West Germany. Originally it was a barbed-wire fence but was later replaced by a five-foot-high cement block wall topped with barbed wire and broken glass. East German soldiers had orders to kill anyone trying to scale the wall.

In November 1989 a surprise move in the wake of a citizens' revolt led to the opening of traffic between East and West Germany and the eventual dismantling of the wall in 1989 and 1990. As the wall was torn down, it became a symbol of the dramatic dismantling of Communism in other parts of the world. With the Cold War over, Busters gained hope that the world would be a safer place.

Peer Groups

As generations grow up, certain institutions shape them into adults. For Builders the strongest influences were family, school, church, and the military. It was within these social institutions that they learned to think, act, and be adults. By the time the Boomers came along, some of these socializing institutions began to lose their influence. Television and college began to have impact.

Once again socializing institutions have changed, and the Busters are learning about life (being socialized) through their peer groups and in the workplace. Often supervision in the workplace is by people not much older than themselves. Many Busters who have faced life in fractured, dysfunctional families have often turned to their peers for support. Para-families, such as gangs, sports teams, and clubs, are helping shape them into adults. Since many have opted to work before going to college, coworkers are important to their developing adulthood.

Music

"I Want to Hold Your Hand" was the first Beatles song to hit the Billboard charts in the United States in January 1964. Listening to that tune today certainly shows that times have changed. Busters' music portrays few illusions about life and love. It may not be more cynical than that of some thirty years ago, but it is less restrained in a culture where almost anything is allowed to be said or sung. Punk rock, heavy metal, and gangsta rap are all types of this new unrestrained music.

Variable Economy

Busters may be inheriting a third-generation rags-to-riches story. Their Builder grandparents rode a developing economy by sacrificing, working hard, and saving. Their Boomer parents have lived through a strong economy, spending the wealth that had accrued. Busters came of age facing a much weaker economy in the 1980s, which made it more difficult to buy a home, pay off a mortgage, even find a job. Busters have also experienced the growth of the technology economy of the 1990s and its slowdown in early 2001. During their life span the percentage of college students pursuing degrees in literature, history, and foreign languages has dropped while one major has increased dramatically—business. Busters are interested in business because it offers the best hope for careers that will be financially profitable. Of course, Busters also wanted to choose a career in a field that would need workers when they were ready to enter the workforce.

Persian Gulf War

On January 15, 1991, when Iraq failed to withdraw its troops from Kuwait, Operation Desert Storm began. U.S. and coalition forces attacked Saddam Hussein's army to force their withdrawal. A prolonged air attack and four days of ground combat were all that were needed to defeat Hussein's army. An estimated 100,000 Iraqi soldiers died in the battle with allied losses totaling fewer than 200.

The Gulf War was different from the Vietnam War in several ways. It was superbly planned and executed. It was short and cost few lives. It was sanctioned by Congress. It was supported by the American public. It was a war we won. Among Busters, this created a positive feeling about the United States and our armed forces.

AIDS

When basketball star Magic Johnson retired from basketball in 1991 due to his being HIV positive, publicity about the AIDS epidemic rose sharply. AIDS (acquired immune deficiency syndrome), a disease of the immune system, is caused by a virus known as HIV (human immunodeficiency virus). First identified in 1981, AIDS has since risen to epidemic proportions throughout the world. Originally found primarily in gay men in urban areas, it has now spread to heterosexual groups throughout the population and has become a social and political issue as well as a health issue. In the United States more litigation cases have arisen as a result of AIDS than any other disease. The World Health Organization estimated that in the year 2000 more than forty million people were infected worldwide.

The effect of the AIDS epidemic on Busters is staggering. They are part of a culture where sex before marriage with multiple partners is accepted and expected, but if they indulge in sex, they know they may get AIDS and die. Never before has a generation had to be so aware of their own mortality.

Oklahoma City Bombing

On April 19, 1995, a terrorist car bomb exploded outside the Alfred P. Murrah Federal Building in Oklahoma City, Oklahoma, leaving 168 people dead and injuring hundreds more. Making the devastation seem worse was the fact that 19 of the dead were children, most of whom had been in the American Kids day care center located in the Murrah building. The attack occurred in the heartland capital city of 440,000, where residents had often joked that it was a "town where nothing much ever happens."

The explosion collapsed the north face of the nine-story concrete building and at the time was described by authorities as the deadliest terrorist attack ever on U.S. soil. Timothy McVeigh, a decorated U.S. Army veteran, was eventually arrested, convicted, and executed for the terrorist attack. He claimed he did it to punish the U.S. government for the deaths of David Koresh and eighty-six members of the Branch Davidian cult on April 19, 1993, in Waco, Texas.

The Oklahoma bombing created a feeling that the world in which we live is not safe. It forced Busters, and all generations, to face the potential danger that exists, even in the United States, from terrorist attack.

Clinton Administration

Young Bill Clinton's excitement about meeting President Kennedy so inspired him that he decided he wanted to become president himself. His excitement was felt by most Boomers who saw the youthfulness of Kennedy, his wife, and family as a sign of hope for the future. Camelot was real, if only for a short while, in the hearts and spirits of the Boomers.

The administration of President Bill Clinton had a similar effect on the minds and spirits of Busters. The twenty-two-year age gap between him and former president George Bush was striking enough to make people take notice. Only John F. Kennedy entered the presidency with a larger age difference—

a twenty-seven-year difference between him and outgoing President Dwight D. Eisenhower.

The mixed messages sent from the Clinton presidency and lifestyle, however, have left an uncertain legacy on the lives of Busters. In 2000 the Clinton presidency ended on a sour note, with the Monica Lewinsky scandal, which broke in 1998, still fresh in the minds of the people. On December 19, 1998, the U.S. House of Representatives approved two articles of impeachment against President Clinton. Two months later, on February 12, 1999, the U.S. Senate failed to convict the president on either charge, leading to an inauspicious ending to his two terms.

Buster Concerns and Characteristics

Members of the Bust generation take their identity as much from what they are not as from what they are. They are not the Boomers, although the line separating them from the Trailing-Edge Boomers is a thin one. There are, however, some dominant themes that seem to characterize various segments of this generation and may be helpful in designing ministry to reach them.

Freedom

Many Busters reject the workaholism often needed to acquire money and titles and to climb the career ladder. They do not expect to make personal sacrifices for the company, and they expect personal satisfaction from their jobs. To them, other interests are as important as work. Flexibility, work-free weekends, and short-term tasks with measurable results are expected.

Freedom also means an openness to changing locations when necessary. According to a U.S. Census Bureau report in 2000, Americans aged twenty to twenty-nine were the top movers between 1998 and 1999. Close to 32 percent—double the national average of 15.9 percent—relocated during the year.

'60s Nostalgia

Busters flock to see Paul McCartney, the Who, and the Beach Boys. As is true of generations before them, they hear about former times and wish they had lived then. The '60s is the era that attracts many Busters. It is far enough removed that the fighting and dying for causes can seem exciting and the life of a hippie romantic. Many Busters like '60s artifacts, such as peace signs.

The most frequently mentioned role model for all Busters is Michael Jordan. After him come people from the past: John F. Kennedy, Elvis Presley, James Dean, and Martin Luther King.

Issues of Survival

National and global issues such as world hunger, homelessness, AIDS, the federal deficit, poverty, and pollution are so large and complex that most people feel helpless to do anything about them. Busters seem to have no illusions about solving these problems, so they tend to focus on issues closer to home where they can see results. Fifty percent of Busters are environmentally conscious and are drawn to groups that have a well-focused message, choose specific targets, and get things accomplished quickly.

Because of problems such as pollution, poverty, AIDS, and the safe disposal of nuclear waste, Busters are very aware that the quality of life on this planet may drastically decline during their lifetime. The accidents at nuclear power plants at Three Mile Island in Pennsylvania and at Chernobyl have forced Busters to put survival goals above self-actualization goals. Busters must deal with the stress of living in an increasingly dangerous world.[4]

Feeling Neglected

More than 40 percent of Busters are children of divorce. They were latchkey kids, which may mean they were neglected by parents who were too occupied with their careers and personal freedom to pay much attention to them. Forty to fifty percent of Busters lived in single-parent homes while teenagers, usually headed by working mothers. Busters are twice as likely to come from broken homes as their Boomer parents and three times as likely as their Builder grandparents.[5] Often Busters are lonely. They plugged into the marvels of communication, but these diversions have isolated them. Walkmans, computers, VCRs, and TVs all created more time alone without interaction with others.

Willing to Work

Young Busters work for the same reasons youth have always worked—for extra spending money, to buy a car, to pay their way through college. Today many are in the workplace rather than at college because they question the value of a college education. Most of the jobs open to those without a college education, however, are low-skilled and low-paying and thus are a negative introduction to the world of work.

Talented Busters are moving into entry-level jobs with no difficulty, but it may be difficult for them to reach higher levels in the job market. For several years, Boomers will block their way to advancement.

The generational stereotype that Busters are lazy, anti-authority slackers has been proven wrong. They are willing to work hard for companies that set high standards regarding work ethic. Yet Busters are not motivated by loftier job titles and more pay. The feeling that they have an impact on the productivity of the business or ministry is what matters to them.

Boomer Values Rejected

Having observed what divorce, career climbing, and drug abuse have done to their Boomer parents, Busters are rejecting many of their parents' values and lifestyles. One clear example is the decline in the appeal of the abortion rights movement to women of this generation. A report published in 1999 revealed that among Buster women, approval of abortion has dropped from a high in 1989 of 65.5 percent to 49.5 percent in 1998.[6]

Forced to grow up too quickly, some of them have even had to "parent" their own parents. They appear to be more conservative and hold more traditional values than their parents do. Although they hope to someday be happily married, many lack relational skills due to the broken and dysfunctional homes in which they were raised.

Practical Education

The high cost of a college education and the competition for good jobs have forced Busters to be very practical about their education. Styles of learning have changed too. Builders were audio learners, willing to sit and listen to lectures. Boomers were visual learners, influenced by television. Busters are also visual learners, but they learn through experience as well. Technically referred to as kinesthetic learners, they want not only to "see" the lesson but to "feel" it.

Growing up in a media-saturated society has instilled in Busters an expectation of immediate satisfaction. The rapid pacing of television and video games gives them the impression that life moves quickly, and they become easily bored when things move slowly. Having grown up in a world with few mundane schedules, Busters find it difficult to complete assignments and projects requiring sequential work.

Postponing Marriage

In 1990 *Time* reported that 75 percent of young adults 18–24 years old still lived at home, the largest number since the Great Depression.[7] As of June 2001, 18 million 20–34 year olds lived at home, or 38 percent of all young adult singles.[8] *Fortune* reported that of men 25–29 years old, 46 percent had never married. Thirty percent of women in that age bracket had never married. In 1970, 19 percent of men in the same age bracket and 11 percent of women had not married.[9] As of 1997 the median age at the time of marriage for Busters was 25 for women and 26.8 for men. In contrast, in 1970 Boomer women were marrying at age 20.8 and Boomer men at 23.2.[10] Busters may be overly cautious about marriage if they have experienced the unhappiness of a broken home. They may also find that they can have satisfying relationships outside of marriage that do not require long-term commitments.

Conclusion

In some ways, Busters have lost out on many of the things their parents and grandparents enjoyed. The economic condition of our country, the threat of environmental problems, and the many broken homes have created an insecure and often hopeless generation. Like all generations before them, only the love of Christ can truly heal their hurts and redeem their lostness.

Busters and the Church | 8

Not long ago it seemed that everyone was talking about the Busters, or Generation X. Cover stories in *U.S. News and World Report, Business Week,* the *New York Times, USA Today, Christianity Today,* and countless new books were coming to terms with the Buster generation.

Early secular writers appeared to write off this 13er generation. Thirteen is a number we try to avoid. Elevators do not stop at the thirteenth floor, donut bakers do not count number thirteen (it's a baker's dozen), and who likes to go out on Friday the thirteenth? Busters have been dismissed as empty, boring, uninspired, cynical, and selfish.

These evaluations may have been accurate a few years ago. But then every generation, when it is young, can be described in these terms. Busters are growing up and so have many of their attitudes and perspectives. Church leaders must overcome past prejudices and begin to reach out to Busters with the acceptance and love commanded by Christ.

Influences on Religious Involvement

"God loves Busters and so do we" would make a good motto for churches during the next twenty years. The church of the 2020s and beyond will be led by Busters, so it is vitally important that we understand and minister to them today. What can we expect as we seek to minister to this generation? Here are a few key insights for consideration.

Importance of Family

Because so many Busters are children of divorced and dysfunctional families, they value a true family atmosphere. Dual-income and workaholic parents often could not or did not take the time to build healthy family relationships with their Buster children. The result has led Busters to place a heavy emphasis on family. Bill Marvel and Melissa Morrison, writing in the *Dallas Morning News,* confirm that "Thirteeners will establish marriages that are far more stable and enduring than those of their oft-divorced parents. And . . . they will become extremely protective parents, seeking to shield their children from the harsh realities they experienced growing up."[1] Family, to Busters, is broadly defined to include practically anyone who will be their friend. Thus a Sunday school class or small group for Busters becomes more than that. It actually becomes family or parafamily.

Local Causes

Compared to their Boomer parents, who when they were young thought they could change the world, Busters are idealists with a small *i*. Busters want to make a difference in the world, but the causes they support are small *c* causes. More pragmatic than the generations before them, they want to be able to see the results of their involvement. Causes close to home attract their interest far more than national or worldwide causes.

Shorter Attention Span

One criticism of Busters is that they are aliterate; that is, they know how to read but choose not to. They are the "sound bite" generation that has been raised on fast-paced television shows and video games. Advertisers discovered a long time ago that the way to get the attention of Busters is to make ads short and full of action. When it comes to church, the slow pace of most services bores Busters. They may sit through the services, all the time knowing they were designed for their parents, not for them. Busters lose interest quickly, and churches that hope to reach them must consider this seriously or there will be fewer Busters in the seats next Sunday.

Up-to-Date Options

Churches that reach Busters for Christ will have innovative services, on the cutting edge technologically and musically.

For Busters, video games, faxes, cellular phones, ATM cards, compact discs, and computers have always been around. A church that does not have computers and the latest in audio-video equipment will seem old-fashioned.

Busters respond to short, pointed dramas that are part of the worship service. Sermons or classes that are straight lectures will not cut it for most members of this generation. Busters learn best through experience and visual images. They respond to sermons delivered close to the audience, rather than from behind a pulpit, removed from the crowd. Illustrations about real people alive today touch their hearts more than stories of people who died long ago in places unfamiliar to them.

Busters also like choice, and larger churches continue to attract a disproportionate number of Busters because they can offer a greater number of choices than smaller churches can. The number of choices Busters have grown up with is mind-boggling. When Boomers were growing up, they had a choice of three major television channels, but Busters have had hundreds of cable channels to choose from. Boomers had a few movie theaters in town, but Busters have a choice of thousands of videos that can be viewed right at home.

Busters have a variety of musical tastes. For some it is rap while for others it is heavy metal or classic rock or jazz. Many like several different styles. Most younger Busters like their music loud and fast with a good beat. Much of the music Busters enjoy today has musical and emotional depth. Songs are experiences they want to feel and lose themselves in. A church that wants to attract Busters must have music that conforms to their standards.

Faith That Meets Needs

A hurting generation always looks for answers, and Busters are no different. Society and school have taught them that there are no absolutes, and yet they long for the solid answers that only personal faith can provide. An absence of good values, the frustration of isolation, and the emptiness of their lives are all leading many Busters on a spiritual search.

First, Busters want their own needs met. Busters are very pragmatic about their faith. They want a faith that works for them. While all generations have had their share of problems, this generation experiences more dysfunctions, abuses, and broken families than any before it. The lack of strong support networks or moral ethics has resulted in a problem-ridden generation. Thus they look for a church that will nurture them and give them practical resources to survive in a post-Christian culture.

Second, Busters want to meet the real needs of other people. They expect churches to be concerned about and involved with the social, political, and environmental issues of their local communities.

Less Structure

Busters have soft hearts not hard hearts. They long to be accepted for who they are and to know that they matter to God. The new currency of life is not money but time. For this generation, free time has become more valuable than money. Thus they do not tend to work overtime or take work home at night. With all the activities and pastimes available to them, Busters are busier than their Boomer parents were at the same age.

With the many demands on the Busters' time, structured church activities are often not top priorities. This means that Busters will probably be at fewer church activities than their Boomer parents. But Busters enjoy unstructured activities and will respond to those who are willing to spend time with them. The best way to touch their hearts for Christ is to simply spend time doing things with them. Taking time to play basketball or a table game will do more to open their hearts to the gospel than will most church services.

Stress

There are few carefree days for Busters. Drugs, AIDS, gangs, terrorism, violence, and crime threaten their well-being. The huge expense of college and the shrinking job market make them pessimistic about their future. And the moral choices that confront them daily keep them constantly on the alert. A *San Francisco Chronicle* poll found that six out of ten Busters feel life is harder for them than for their parents. Twenty-five percent of Buster women say their lives are "very stressful." Three of ten think that all the good jobs have been taken. Older Busters see Boomers holding all the good jobs, and they figure they will have five to ten years at the end of their careers when these jobs will be available to them.[2] They need help dealing with the stress and not a religion that piles on more burdens. Their faith needs to answer the YBH question—yes, but how? A religion full of "oughts" and "shoulds" will be rejected for one that provides the "whats" and "hows."

According to Scripture, Jesus was a man acquainted with grief, but he came to offer us abundant life. Many Busters have experienced grief in their short lives. Many have had unhappy home lives, and some have experienced the death of friends through suicide, drugs, or AIDS. They look for faith that is uplifting and a religion that accommodates great dreams and makes room for laughter.

Ministering to Busters

Busters are beginning to make their voices heard. Perhaps a new name is appropriate for them—the Re-Generation.

The Re-Generation is tired of feeling disenfranchised, disconnected, and overshadowed. They are beginning to step forward and take command of their lives. Alert church leaders need to step forward themselves and reach out in ministry to this Re-Generation. Here are some ideas.

Define Vision

Busters tend to prefer churches that have a clear focus, a narrowly defined vision, and a commitment to accomplish their mission. A mission statement such as "to know Christ and make him known" may be too theoretical to be relevant to Busters. A pragmatic generation, Busters want to know exactly where and how such a mission will be carried out. How are we actually going to get to know Christ? To whom exactly is the church trying to make Christ known? Busters also need to see evidence that members are involved in ministries that accomplish their mission.

Keep Worship Authentic

Churches that have honest, straightforward, tell-it-like-it-is worship services seem to attract Busters. Worship services can be short or long, just so they are real and not considered a waste of time. Very time conscious, Busters want to get on to the next project or activity in their lives. They need to feel that the church values their time and does not ask them to attend a service that is too long and is poorly designed or conducted.

Most Busters grew up thinking that church is boring. This was probably more because of the pace of worship than the content of the church service. Busters are not bored by worship but by services that move slowly.

Music is important to most Busters, and the generation has varied tastes. If a church is trying to attract Busters, up-to-date music and a variety of styles should be included in the worship service. Buster members should be involved in the selection and performance of the music.

Busters expect those who conduct a church service to strive for excellence. This MTV generation practically grew up with remote controls in their hands. If a TV show did not hold their attention, they switched channels. Though they cannot do this during a worship service that does not meet their standards, they do feel free to "switch channels" and attend another church.

Focus on Local Issues

Busters tend to prefer churches that focus on local ministry rather than ministry in faraway places. In this they are like their Boomer parents. They will volunteer to tutor school children and feed the hungry at a local soup kitchen. They will minister to the homeless or elderly in their own community. But they are seldom inspired to work for a ministry that is far from them geographically or philosophically. One important issue that attracts their attention and involvement is the environment. Anything a church can do to help improve the environment in their community will likely gain the support of Busters.

Busters will give money to churches when they can see their investment is bringing results. They like to know that their money is changing the lives of real people. During worship services interviews with people who have been touched with the ministry of your church lets Buster members hear the results of their investment. Using videos of interviews or short CNN-style reports are powerful ways to demonstrate the fruit of ministry.

Challenge to Short-Term Service

Busters are likely to volunteer for short-term ministry activities. The general rule is "recruit for the short-term and renew for the long-term." As with young people of every generation, Busters resist long-term commitments. So the best approach is to start small. Busters do need discipling in this area, however, so they can learn to make longer commitments. Once they have experienced success in ministry, invite them to sign on for a slightly longer time period.

Disciple through Small Groups

Busters usually enjoy the interaction of small groups. They need the encouragement and feedback of a few people they can trust. Leaders need to watch for those who have difficulty applying general concepts to their own lives. For example, they may need help in recognizing who in their lives is their neighbor whom they should love. Some will need specific, step-by-step instructions and accountability. A small group is the best place for this to take place.

Answer Questions

Busters often need to sort out the hurts in their lives. Churches can help them do this through practical messages, classes, and small groups. Church leaders, especially those who preach and teach, need to get to know Busters and identify their felt needs. One-on-one interviews and small-group discussions are good ways to find out what they are thinking and where they are hurting. In general, they are concerned with anything dealing with relationships, being successful in life, and healing inner pain from their childhood years. In this they may not be very different from church members of other generations, but because they are young, the problems they face every day—sexual immorality, pornography, child abuse, drug and alcohol abuse, sexually transmitted disease, divorce, AIDS—can seem overwhelming. They need honest answers to their questions so they know how to deal with these issues.

Develop Need-Based Ministry

The fastest growing ministries in the United States over the past decade have been support ministries. Support groups and classes on topics like divorce care, overcoming addictions, and surviving abuse attract a large number of participants. Even one-day workshops on topics such as these will usually be well attended. Busters will be attracted to churches through need-based ministries that deal with the hurts and issues they are facing.

Conclusion

It is critical that we begin to understand the driving forces in the lives of Busters. If we hope to minister to them in our church, we need to be, to paraphrase an advertising slogan, "just slightly ahead of our time."

Reaching Busters

9

Busters are experiencing the standard transitions of life. Their top concerns at this point of life include having a good marriage and family, choosing a career, being successful in work, having strong friendships, paying for college, having a prosperous country, making a lot of money, finding purpose and meaning in life, and staying healthy. These are basically the same issues that every generation has been concerned with at their age.

Christ has the answer to the concerns of Busters, but they are not asking the question in quite the way that previous generations have. As noted previously, 65 percent of Builders and 35 percent of Boomers say they are believers in Christ. The research by Dr. Thom Rainer, noted previously, concluded that only 15 percent of Busters have been reached for Christ. Being one of the least churched generations to come along, they are not looking to the church for discussion, let alone answers.

A study that was reported in June 2001 found that young adults aged eighteen to twenty-nine are the least likely to attend church. In a one week period, the Gallup organization found that 33 percent of those eighteen to twenty-nine years old attended church, while 40 percent of thirty to sixty-four year olds and 52 percent of sixty-five to seventy-four year olds attended.[1]

As a church strives to design a strategy to reach unchurched Busters, it should keep the following five concepts in mind.

1. *Physically, nothing captivates Busters more than sports and fitness.* They watch sports, play games, exercise, and stay even more fit than their Boomer parents. This is as true of women as men. Buster women have been the first generation to participate to a large extent in competitive athletics while in high school. While in junior high, high school, and college, many Busters saw both men and women competing in swimming, weight lifting, soccer, volleyball, basketball, softball, and other sports. Gymnasiums are sure to become as important for churches that want to reach out to Busters as their sanctuaries are.

2. *Relationally, nothing captivates Busters more than friends and family.* As noted, friends are often the family of Busters. Even if their biological family lives apart from them, they will still have a sense of belonging and roots if they have friends. They are like all of us in that they need to belong and be loved, and they need to know that they are loved and appreciated for who they are more than for what they do. Involvement with friends in family-style activities, like dinners, parties, and holiday celebrations, appeals to them. Group discussions centered on topics that families might discuss over dinner—what happened at work or school, local or national events, plans for the future, the pastor's message—are popular.

3. *Mentally, nothing captivates Busters more than entertainment and music.* Over their brief history Busters as a group have seen more movies, plays, sports events, concerts, and television than any other generation. They like to be entertained.

4. *Socially, nothing captivates Busters more than improving the environment.* Oil spills, the burning of rain forests, and the dangers of nuclear waste are documented on television on a regular basis. The Busters have not only heard about these problems, but they have experienced them personally through the television screen. As school children and youth they wrote reports on the protection of dolphins, owls, fish, and eagles.

They realize the necessity of recycling. They fear that before they really have time to enjoy it, our earth may be destroyed. So, to them, protection of the environment is critical.

5. *Spiritually, nothing captivates Busters more than a search for serenity.* Busters have been dazzled with the numbers and types of technological innovations developed during their lifetime. From computers to cellular phones to Game Boys, they have become accustomed to products that make life easier and/or entertain. However, Busters are finding that the fruits of technology can isolate people. They are seekers looking for truth and are open to churches that will show them how to go about their search.

Reaching Unchurched Busters

Clark Morphew, a writer for Knight-Ridder Newspapers, sums up the opportunity for churches who wish to reach unchurched Busters with the gospel. He advises, "Teach these people how to pray, meditate and relax and they will stick with you forever. Ignore their spiritual needs and they will drift away in search of serenity in all the wrong places."[2]

Keep in mind that a one-size-fits-all approach to ministry will not work with Busters. They are a diverse group, and successful ministry to them will depend greatly on the age group, social background, and even geographic location of your Busters. You will have to experiment to find the best activities for the Busters you are trying to reach. Be ready to try new approaches. Here are some tips for churches that seriously wish to reach Busters with the good news of Jesus Christ.

Become a Buster-Friendly Church

Looking at churches from the Busters' point of view, there are three styles of churches: Buster-centered, Buster-friendly, and Buster-hostile. A Buster-centered church greets Busters with an excited "Welcome, we've prepared this church just for you." A Buster-friendly church greets Busters with a friendly

"We thought you might drop by. Come on in and enjoy yourself." A Buster-hostile church greets Busters with a disgruntled "What are you doing here?"

Not every church can or should be Buster-centered. That approach is for churches that feel called to target Busters exclusively. Every church should be a Buster-friendly church, however. Every church should prepare for and expect that Busters will drop by. Some churches will remain Buster-hostile and, if they are also Boomer-hostile, they will not be with us for too many more years.

Remember that unchurched Busters are already predisposed to not like church, so to be a Buster-friendly church you must begin to do the following:

- Play down titles and use first names.
- Eliminate churchy sounding words like *foyer, vestibule,* and *sanctuary* and replace them with common terms like *platform, auditorium,* and *lobby.*
- Provide excellent child-care facilities. You may find about 40 percent of your Busters are still unmarried, but those that are married and have children will want superior facilities for their children.
- Explain everything you do, so unchurched Busters will have some idea of what is going on.
- Use the style of music they listen to in their cars and at home.
- Dress casually.
- Remodel the church so that it reflects contemporary colors, fabrics, and styles. Obviously a church cannot remodel every year, but put in place a plan that allows for remodeling at least every five years so that unchurched people will not view your church as outdated.
- Install equipment that Busters expect, such as Power Point projectors and computers.
- Do not call attention to Buster guests. Welcome visitors as a group, invite them to sit back and enjoy the service, and

direct them to a welcome center for further information and refreshments.

Value Busters

Busters have found very little in our world that is directed specifically to them as a group. Their Boomer parents may have ignored them as they pursued careers. Traditional churches have ignored them, preferring to minister to the Builder generation. It's surprising, but even seeker-oriented churches have reached out primarily to Boomers and ignored Busters. As a result, many unchurched Busters feel lonely and neglected and are looking for some person, group, or institution that will love and value them. Churches that take time to understand Busters, and then minister to them, will find Busters very responsive. This will involve such things as

- a worship service just for them using their music
- sermons, seminars, and workshops that touch on the needs they are facing
- scheduling that fits their lifestyles
- support groups that help them heal their hurts
- opportunities for them to develop relationships
- an atmosphere that helps them experience their faith
- a dress code that is relaxed
- teaching that focuses on the basics of the Christian faith, avoiding Christian clichés
- programming for singles, young couples, and families
- extending a welcome that overlooks nonconformity and allows for appropriate tolerance in all of life's arenas

Start a New Worship Service

Begin a worship service targeted to Busters who may be seeking the Lord or at least answers to their spiritual needs. Be sure to do the following.

- Choose the best time. Busters typically like a church service that starts between 9:00 and 10.00 A.M. However, some churches are finding success in reaching them with a Saturday or Sunday evening worship service. Some careful research will help you determine the best time for a service in your particular area.
- Make a good first impression. Busters are unsure about churches in the first place. They will make a decision about your church within thirty seconds of entering the front door, so make that first thirty seconds good.
- Keep things relaxed. Eliminate any aspect of the service that is not absolutely necessary if it might place undue pressure on the Buster.
- Be positive. Help Busters see the joy in serving Christ.
- Use a response card. Never ask Busters to walk forward or stand up or raise their hand to indicate any personal decisions. Instead, ask them to indicate a decision on a response card. You will get a better response and not alienate Busters already scared of church.
- Be real. Do not sugarcoat sermons or messages. Be gracious, but tell it like it is.

In addition, you may want to think about the following ministries.

- Start a drama ministry. Drama allows you to remove barriers by drawing Busters into the theme of the message and raising questions that you will answer in your message. The actors should be close in age to the Busters in the audience. Drama works well with Busters because they are media-oriented. Even though a drama ministry can be effective, it's better to have no drama than to present bad drama. Begin by performing one drama per month and then work up to a weekly presentation as the talent surfaces.
- Develop a video production team. Start a CTN (Church Television Network) or a WTN (Worship Television Net-

work) or an MTN (Ministry Television Network). Use video to produce documentaries about people who have had their lives touched by Jesus and your church. Produce a seven- to ten-minute introductory video about your church and the ministries you have to offer. Give every prospective Buster a copy. At the very least, project the words to your music via computer projection. Whatever you do, pack up the hymnbooks and put them away.

Preach "How to" Messages

Busters are looking for messages that tell them how to be successful in life. Sermon titles such as "How to Raise a Happy Family" or "How to Develop Loving Relationships" will often draw many listeners. Before delivering a message to Busters, you should be able to give the "take away" value in one statement.

Messages should relate to one of the following three areas: relationships, purpose in life, or healing emotional scars. Be real and approachable. Use honest and up-to-date illustrations that show how to find an answer or deal with a specific problem. Use the practical part of the message to lead into the spiritual part. For example, begin with human relationships and bridge into relationship with God. It seems easier to reach Busters through the heart rather than the head, through emotions rather than the mind. But be sure to talk *with* them, not *down to* them.

Educators tell us that people have different learning styles. Busters learn best experientially. As they participate in activities and get involved emotionally, they receive the most benefit from the teaching.

Leaders and teachers of small groups, classes, and seminars must take the Busters' learning style seriously. Creative teaching techniques that involve the learner in the process will produce better results and application than simple lecturing. While some lecture is needed in classes and seminars, teachers should always build in an experiential component. Pastors can involve the audience experientially in the messages with carefully chosen illustrations, rhetorical questions, and drama.

In all cases, remember that many Busters have had less church background and have less biblical knowledge than their Boomer parents or Builder grandparents. Much of what they hear in a sermon may be new to them. They may take longer to assimilate information and will respond with the YBH question—"Yes, but how?"

Busters tend to be visual learners, rather than cognitive learners. When information is not presented in a visual form, it may take them longer to digest. Never assume Busters know how to put the message into practice. Tell them how to do it in precise, practical terms. Every lecture, message, and presentation must include the exact steps for implementation or application.

Establish New Ministries

The churches that effectively reach and win unchurched Busters almost always do so by starting something new rather than modifying an existing program or ministry. Starting a new group, a new ministry, a new worship service, and in a lot of situations, a brand-new church, is often needed to reach unchurched Busters.

Large group activities where Busters can get together in groups of fifteen to thirty people work well. Sports activities are good for this and also evening discussion groups. Guest speakers with special expertise can be invited. For Busters who lack the people skills needed in small-group settings, larger groups may be the answer. They provide a party atmosphere that Busters appreciate, especially if music is included.

Churches have used sports in the past as a form of fellowship for their church members. Sports and recreation are often successfully used to reach unchurched Busters. Find out what recreational activities are popular with Busters in your area and put together outings or teams to attract them. These activities can be for both men and women and might include volleyball, softball, basketball, aerobics, biking, golf, racquetball, mountain climbing, and hiking.

You may want to consider scheduling retreats for various groups of Busters. Youth leaders understand that one of the best places to reach teenagers for Christ is at a camp. When people are removed from their normal everyday environment, they begin to relax and think about issues that usually never cross their minds. It is in these relaxed camp settings that many youth find Christ.

A similar possibility exists when Busters are away for a retreat. A retreat will attract unchurched Busters if it is built around sports activities, such as skiing, boating, or mountain climbing, or if there is a special speaker on a topic of interest. Comfortable accommodations and good food should be provided. Be sure to treat your Buster guests as adults.

Provide Parafamily Structures

For many Busters, a Buster-friendly church may become closer to them than family. Developing parafamily structures, such as small groups for singles, young marrieds, and single parents will often meet needs for support and advice.

Other parafamily structures include sports teams, worship teams, small informal gatherings, and task-oriented committees. Parafamily structures can be small—from two or three up to six or eight. If they are much larger, they often cease to function as a family structure, and there is not as much opportunity for personal attention.

Teach Life Skills

It is in families that most people learn life skills, such as how to manage money, care for others, discipline themselves, and manage their time. These skills are needed to get along well in life. The broken family and dysfunctional background of many Busters has left them with a lack of training in these traditional skills. Churches can meet these needs and reach out to unchurched Busters at the same time. Short, two- or three-hour seminars on topics such as "How to Get Along with Difficult People," "How to Make a Budget," and "How to Manage Your Time" will often attract Busters who are struggling in these areas. To get started, you should survey unchurched Busters in your church's ministry area to discover their concerns. Then develop a short workshop and advertise it where they are sure to see the advertisement (not in the church program). During the workshop, do not preach at them. Give them an honest workshop on the topic advertised. Your goal is not to bring people to Christ through this type of workshop but to help them get to know and trust the people of your church and to help them feel comfortable coming to your church building.

Be Involved in the Community

If a church wishes to meet and reach the Busters of its community, it should become involved in community projects. Working together helps build trust between Christians and the Busters who get involved. Busters are often interested in projects having to do with kids from broken homes, homelessness, unemployment, and the environment. Your church might organize groups to paint the homes of elderly people or be big brothers and sisters, host a monthly birthday party, or provide tutoring or music lessons for needy children. Become involved in substance abuse meetings and recovery groups that are open to the community at large.

Stress Marriage and Family

Busters are more like their grandparents than their parents when it comes to the value they place on family. Busters are often interested in how to make family relationships work. Provide classes, workshops, and retreats for training in marriage and family development. Sponsor family outings or special events about every six weeks.

Many Busters may have grown up in dysfunctional families and plan to do better by their own children, but Busters will still adopt many of the values and opinions of their parents. There is far more congruence than conflict between the views of Boomers and Busters. Many Busters need to learn the skill of conflict resolution, and for many the first conflict to resolve will be with their parents. While this cannot and should not be forced, it can be encouraged appropriately. When Busters see restored relationships among their peers and their families, this is a powerful testimony.

Provide Quality Child Care and Education Programs

Busters expect a well-structured education program for their elementary-aged children, using up-to-date materials and methods. Replace enclosed Sunday school rooms with learning centers.

For infants provide a well-equipped nursery that is comparable to a baby's room at home. Busters want a church nursery to provide the same quality care they would find at the best weekday care centers. Churches hoping to reach Busters should improve church nurseries with good lighting, new carpeting, clean toys, and bright colors. In addition, nurseries should be accessible and well staffed, with well thought-out policies.

Communicate Your Vision

Communicate the purpose and vision of your church with concrete examples of what is meant. Since people tend to lose sight of a vision within about two weeks, tell them over and over in various ways and with different examples. As a rule, mention the direction of your church at least biweekly and tie it directly to a practical result or ministry that you are involved with at the present. Communicate effectively by using video, newsletters, cards, and drama.

Offer Time and Space

Busters are seekers on a spiritual pilgrimage, and their pilgrimage is likely to last longer than those of earlier generations. This is true for several reasons. First, they are the first post-Christian generation, so many of them lack the foundation of a Judeo-Christian upbringing. There is a lot of groundwork that must be laid before they can make a commitment to Christ. Second, they carry many hurts that will need healing before they can move on to another phase of their lives. Third, they learn by experimenting, and it takes time to experiment. Fourth, since they have not grown up in the church, they are predisposed to think the church is irrelevant. Patience, flexibility, and love are the ingredients needed to build a ministry to this unchurched generation.

Conclusion

Most researchers agree that Busters are a hurting generation. Pastor Dieter Zander planted NewSong church in Southern California in order to reach the emerging Buster generation. Within six years, NewSong grew to more than twelve hundred worshipers with an average age of twenty-six. Zander's study and experience with Busters confirmed that the Busters' main needs are relationships, purpose in life, and personal healing.

Many Busters are already a generation removed from the church. They do not understand it and may think it is irrelevant. Yet some churches are reaching out to unchurched Busters and finding success in touching their hearts for Christ. These churches tend to focus on the needs and pain of Busters and thereby build bridges to them to share the gospel of Jesus Christ. Churches that heal hurts and build bridges will touch the lives of Busters.

The Buster Generation

Aliases	Yiffies (young, individualistic, freedom-minded, and few)
	13ers (13th generation from the founding fathers)
	Posties (Post-Boomer generation)
	Generation X
	Echo Boom
	Baby Boomlet
	The Reagan generation
Formative Years	1980s, 1990s, and 2000s
Formative Experiences	*Roe v. Wade*
	High technology
	Video games and television
	The *Challenger* disaster
	Berlin Wall dismantled
	Peer groups and work
	Music, music, music
	Variable economy
	Persian Gulf War
	AIDS
	Oklahoma City bombing
	Clinton administration
Concerns and Characteristics	Freedom
	'60s nostalgia
	Community causes
	Feel neglected and lonely
	Willing to work
	Boomer values rejected
	Practical education desired
	Postponing marriage
Religious Characteristics	Committed to family
	Local causes
	Shorter attention span
	Want up-to-date options
	Want faith that meets needs
	Want less structure
	Need to relieve stress
Buster Ministry	Define vision
	Update worship service
	Focus on local issues

Challenge to short-term service
Use small groups
Answer questions
Develop need-based ministries

Common Needs and Interests

Sports and fitness
Friends and family
Entertainment and music
Improving the environment
Search for serenity

Reaching Unchurched Busters

Become Buster-friendly
Value Busters
Start a seeker service
Preach "how-to" messages
Establish new ministries
Provide parafamily structures
Teach life skills
Be involved in the community
Host large-group activities
Schedule retreats
Stress marriage and family
Provide quality child-care and education programs
Communicate your vision
Offer time and space

Part 4

The Bridger Wave

When Did the Bridgers Arrive?

Move over, Boomers and Busters. There is a new generation waiting in the wings, a generation that is technically skilled, community-minded, and open to change to a greater extent than any previous generation.

Business leaders dub them Generation E, as in future entrepreneurs. Others call them the Ritalin generation, due to the fact that 2.5 million Bridgers took (or continue to take) the drug for ADD (attention deficit disorder). In fact the use of Ritalin doubled during the decade of the 1990s as the oldest of this new generation grew up. A descriptive name for this generation is Mosaics, which points to the fact that they are a heterogeneous generation of views, tastes, beliefs, and ethnicity. NetGen points out that they are the first generation to grow up with the technology of the Internet. Smorgasbord generation refers to the full schedule of choices and activities that compete for this generation's time. Whether it is soccer, computer classes, ballet lessons, or a host of other opportunities, this generation has a smorgasbord of choices. Since many

Bridgers are children of Boomers, the name Echo Boomerang expresses their relationship to the first Baby Boom. Others call them the Always-On generation due to their love of the computer. One of the most popular names is Generation Y, which is the logical extension beyond the older Generation X. Another popular name is Millennials, placing them at the forefront of the twenty-first century. The November 12, 2001, issue of *Newsweek* called them Generation 9-11 due to the dynamic impact produced by the terrorist attack on New York City on September 11, 2001.

For our purposes, the name Bridgers will be used, describing this generation that is coming of age in the transition from the twentieth to the twenty-first century. Literally they are the *bridge* into the new millennium. The term *Bridgers* was introduced by Thom S. Rainer in his book *The Bridger Generation.* Since we named the previous generations Builders, Boomers, and Busters, the use of the name Bridger allows for a memorable alliteration, while accurately describing their transition between two centuries and two millennia.

Born between 1984 and 2002, the Bridgers are the children and/or grandchildren of the Boomers and children of the older Busters.[1] They will represent nearly 74.7 million people by the end of 2002 or 27 percent of the U.S. population. Immigration will swell their number to nearly 76.5 million.

Bridger Births					
1984	3,669,000	1991	4,111,000	1998	3,942,000
1985	3,761,000	1992	4,065,000	1999	3,959,000
1986	3,757,000	1993	4,000,000	2000	4,065,000
1987	3,809,000	1994	3,979,000	2001	3,935,000 est.
1988	3,910,000	1995	3,900,000	2002	3,935,000 est.
1989	4,021,000	1996	3,915,000		
1990	4,158,000	1997	3,881,000		

Like the generations before them, Busters cannot be described as a single unit, but are represented by at least two subgroups: the GenYs and Millennials.

Generation Y

The first portion of the Bridger generation was born between 1984 and 1993. Today they are nine to eighteen years old and represent forty million people. They are comfortable with diversity and wonder if absolute truth exists.

Millennials

The Millennials were born from 1994 through the end of 2002. Currently they are between the ages of one and eight years old and it is estimated that there will be thirty-five million persons in the Millennial cohort. They are one of the most supervised generations to come along in some time and take for granted living in a point, click, view, interactive world.

Bridgers remain too young for many of their generation to have made major impacts on society. Most of them are influenced by members of the Buster generation. Britney Spears, JLo (Jennifer Lopez), Dr. Dre, *NSYNC, Puff Daddy, the Back Street Boys, and Christina Aguilera are musical influences. Haley Joel Osment, who starred in two highly rated movies, is one member of this generation who has begun to make a mark, as is Leslie Carter. Bridgers who are interested in sports often look to golfer Tiger Woods as a model, while basketball players talk of Shaquille O'Neal and Kobe Bryant, and moviegoers admire Ben Affleck.

Formative Experiences

Generations cannot be understood apart from the events or milieu that form their character. Life-shaping events are easier to define after a generation has grown older. Tracing a characteristic back to a probable cause seems more accurate than attempting to predict the future. A Chinese proverb declares, "To prophesy is difficult, especially with regards to the future."

But from today's vantage point, the following events and experiences appear to have impacted the Bridger generation.

Postmodern Era

The beginning date of the postmodern era is difficult to nail down. While the roots of postmodernism were seeded as far back as Kierkegaard and Nietzsche, the fruit became visible in the 1980s and 1990s.

The modern world was based on the premise that through observation and experimentation one could discover knowledge. Logical, linear thinking was the rule. By using the scientific method of thesis, analysis, and research, one could find and know truth. Once the truth was discovered, it could be used to create cures for diseases or explain the supernatural or solve human problems. Thus the modern world was a world of hope and progress.

The postmodern world no longer accepts truth at face value. According to postmodern thinking, all acts and knowledge should be called into question. Globalization has led to the notion that there are multiple correct truths to any question. The shift in worldviews looks to new styles of processing information. For example:

holistic thinking: a comprehensive framework of categories that are interlinked

chunking: processing clusters of information by sticking them into a large, preexisting framework

divergent thinking: working under the notion that a problem may have multiple "correct" or acceptable answers

multitasking: performing several thinking/activity tasks simultaneously

complexification: recognizing that solutions to problems tend to be multifaceted, with interactive layers of factors

paradoxicalism: accepting that two apparently contradictory things can and do coexist *intuition:* trusting "gut-level feelings" and conclusions, even if there is no traditionally logical explanation to how you arrive at the conclusion[2]

Thus the postmodern world is one where value is placed on diversity, justice, and tolerance of multiple points of view. Truth is found by giving serious consideration to inclusive, interactive, complex systems of thought.

Technology/Internet

The society in which Bridgers have grown up is computer dependent. That's why we were all so worried about entering the new millennium, afraid that a computer glitch would send our lives into chaos. It didn't happen, but the potential for disaster let us know what a hold computers have on our well-being. This is all Bridgers have ever known. Life without computers is unimaginable. Not only are there now eighty million computers in our country but they are more powerful than ever.

Computer cost-effectiveness rose 100 millionfold from 1958 to 1997, that is, computers were 100,000 times more powerful and 1,000-fold less costly. Frank Feather, global business futurist and author of *future consumer.com*, writes, "Today, a brand new PC is switched on for the first time in human history every second, 24 hours a day non-stop around the world."[3]

To most of us, it may seem like the Internet has been around forever, but in fact it has been only in the last four years that terms like *dot-com* and *URL* have become mainstream. The Internet is growing at a faster rate than any previous communications medium. For example, it took radio thirty-eight years and television thirteen years from their inception to reach fifty million users in North America. It took the Internet only five years to reach fifty million users. It is suggested that at this rate of growth 64 percent of North American households will be on-line by 2005, 79 percent by 2010! As of May 2000 it was estimated that eleven million domain names were registered for the Internet with fifteen thousand new names registered each day. By 2003 approximately 140 million domain names will have been registered.

More cell phones than computers are sold every year. By 2003 there will be more than one billion cell phones with half of them connected to the Internet. *American Demographics* reported in January 2001 that one-quarter of Bridgers owned cell phones.

Variety of Music

In the past, music solidified teens by offering a common perception of life during their formative years. Music both separates and unites today's teenagers. As we enter the twenty-first century, musical taste is extremely fragmented. Loyalty is divided among such styles as hip hop, rap, alternative, metal, techno, house, pink, reggae, R&B, country, classic rock, and swing.

This variety goes beyond the music to include the language, fashion, activities, friends, and attitudes corresponding to their taste in music.

MTV

On August 1, 2001, MTV celebrated its twentieth anniversary. During the life of Bridgers, this cable television network has had a far-reaching impact on their taste in music, movies, TV, and fashion.

Known for its intoxicating and addicting series of music videos, MTV used the mini-epics to tell stories in four minutes that would take thirty to sixty minutes on traditional television. As a niche network, MTV targeted thirteen to thirty-four year olds. When young audiences tuned in, Hollywood and corporations such as Gap, Tommy Hilfiger, and others began tapping into Bridger tastes by aping the MTV style. For better or worse, the Bridger generation has been influenced by Madonna, *Beavis and Butt-head,* and *MTV Unplugged.*

Diversity

The population of the United States grew by more people in the last decade than any other ten-year period in U.S. history. Swelling by 32.7 million people, the recent population growth was fueled in part by waves of new immigrants and a steady birth rate that outpaced deaths.

As a result, the newest generation of Americans is more racially and ethnically diverse than previous ones. Minorities make up a larger proportion of Bridgers than they do of former generations. Thirty-three percent of Bridgers are minorities compared to 27 percent of the total population, according to the Census Bureau in 2000. When compared to other generations, diversity breaks down as follows:

	White	Minority
Builders	82.2%	17.8%
Boomers	74.9%	25.1%
Busters	68.5%	31.5%
Bridgers	66.8%	33.2%

Columbine

On the morning of April 20, 1999, Columbine High School, located in Littleton, Colorado, was the scene of a mass shooting attack by students Eric Harris and Dylan Klebold. What has become known as the worst school shooting in U.S. history took place on an otherwise normal high school campus. Students throughout the United States watched in horror the news coverage of the event, which created a feeling similar to the effect of the political assassinations on the Boomers. While some students felt the Columbine High shootings were given too much attention by the media, many students began to feel unsafe at school. Some even began to believe that they have the right to protect themselves and considered carrying guns to school.

Longer Life Span

In 1900 the median age of our population was about twenty-three years. In 2000 the median age had risen to about thirty-five. The proportion of people over sixty-five has tripled since 1900 from 4.1 percent to 12.7 percent. According to U.S. census projections, sometime around 2050 people over fifty years old will be the majority of adults in the United States. An older population may mean a world that is less competitive, less isolated, less harsh, less materialistic, and less gullible.

More important, however, is the increasing scale of our lives. For instance, a twenty year old in 1900 would have had only about twenty-five years to build a career, rear a family, and come to terms with death. A twenty year old in today's world may have fifty years ahead in which to do the same. Our youngest generation is likely to stay healthier and work longer than earlier generations, with plenty of time to enjoy life and make a difference in their world.

Speed Is King

Businesses must move from an idea to the marketplace with projects in less than four months time. The reason? That is the estimated time of survival in the fast-paced world of the web, because when a new idea is developed on the Internet, it is outpaced by something even newer in a short time. The mantra of the twenty-first century is "Run fast, but don't miss a step."

Thomas Middelhoff, chairman of Bertelsmann AG, writes, "We have nothing less than industrial revolution. That makes it necessary to change how we see and run our business. That means Speed is King."[4] In the do-or-die deadline world of the Internet, rule breakers are honored, and creativity is respected. Writes Neil Weintraut of 21st Century Internet Venture Partners, "If you have an idea, you have to act on it now. With the Internet, an idea has no time to evolve. It has to happen now."[5]

Customized Lifestyles

The American Dream used to revolve around personal home ownership, a lifelong job, and a secure family. As we move into the twenty-first century, this cookie-cutter vision of life is changing to reflect a customized or individual way of looking at life. No standardized American dream exists. Each individual is customizing a personal dream tailored to his or her interests.

For example, days are carefully organized (customized) for younger people around school, play dates, ballet lessons, horseback riding, and an assortment of other time-consuming activities.

Another form of customization is seen in advertisers using a magazine-catalog hybrid, or "magalog," to reach the new generation. This generation seemingly is bored just looking at standard catalog pictures. So, in an effort to hold their attention, magalogs combine stories with the usual product information. Magalogs offer everything from music reviews to advice on travel to tips on making CD-ROM movies.

Customization is reaching all areas of life, even fashion. The fashion industry has to reinvent itself nearly every six months to keep up with the latest expectations of the new generation.

Terrorist Attacks

On the morning of September 11, 2001, terrorists hijacked and crashed two airliners into the World Trade Center in New York City. Thousands of private citizens were killed as the twin, 110-story towers tumbled to the ground within about ninety minutes after the crashes. A plane also slammed into the Pentagon, while another crashed into an open field short of its intended target.

Widely declared to be America's second Pearl Harbor, the attacks resulted in the temporary closure of all airports within the United States and eventually led to a drop in the stock market as businesses and people struggled to make sense of the event.

President George W. Bush declared war on terrorism and the United States military began a siege on the Taliban leaders in Afghanistan, believing they harbored the terrorist cells responsible for the attacks.

While the long-term effects of the terrorist attacks are difficult to predict, it seems clear that they will be to the Bridger generation what Pearl Harbor was to the Builders and the assassination of John F. Kennedy was to the Boomers.

Characteristics

The Bridger generation is still young, of course, so it is difficult to make a final determination of what will ultimately characterize them. The formative years for the younger half of the generation will continue for several more years. A Bridger generational mystique does appear to be developing, one that will mature, to be sure. The following characteristics can be identified as contributing to this mystique.

Entrepreneurial

It is impossible, of course, to track all the baby-sitters and lawn cutters, but experts note that today's youngest generation seems more inclined to go into business than did past generations. Dr. Marilyn Kourilsky, a Boomer and vice president of the Center for Entrepreneurial Leadership in Kansas City, writes, "A Peace Corps mentality also comes with that entrepreneurial spirit. They feel obligated to give back to the community. I find that different from my generation. I call them generation E."[6]

Part of this may be due to the fact that parents are giving more power to the Bridgers. As of 1999, 70 percent of mothers worked outside the home compared to only 20 percent in the 1950s. This has caused the United States to move from a patriarchy to a matriarchy to a filiarchy, where a great deal of power is given to kids.

Boomers remember struggling with their parents in what became known as a generation gap. In an effort to keep bridges built between them and their children, Boomers have had a strong desire to be friends with their children rather than authority figures. This has given more power to their Buster and Bridger children. Today parents see their children as much more advanced than they were at the same age. This encourages parents to give more authority and responsibility to their children.

Another thing driving the Bridgers' entrepreneurial spirit is the fear that the job market will not be open to them when they reach adulthood. Bridgers believe that many of the advantages the economy offered to previous generations have slipped over to the global economy, and they think jobs that future Americans will be qualified to hold have gone overseas.

Technologically Savvy

Being a Bridger means you need e-mail (which means you need a computer, preferably your own) and a cell phone. Some may still use a pager, but really only Busters still use pagers! A December 2001 report by *American Demographics* magazine declares that 64 percent of Bridgers use cell phones mainly for personal calls, compared with 43 percent of the total population who use cell phones for this purpose.[7] About 36 percent of Bridgers say they regularly use a home computer and 63 percent say they would rather go on-line than watch television. Very few of them read books.

Bridgers have adopted the Internet for numerous activities— 96 percent for sending and receiving e-mail. According to Forrester Research, in 2000 the percentage of Bridgers using the Internet for various purposes was as follows:

Send or receive e-mail	96%
Send or receive instant messages	69%
Download software	63%
Play on-line games	59%

Download music	54%
Read news	52%
Listen to music/radio on-line	49%
Search for jobs	42%
Research products	41%
Purchase products	40%[8]

Neotraditional

"One of the macro-trends we're seeing is neotraditionalism," says Kristy Doig, vice president of Youth Intelligence, a trend forecasting group based in New York City. Bridgers "are fed up with the superficialities of life. They have not had a lot of stability in their lives. It's a backlash, a return to tradition and ritual. And that includes marriage. It's all about finding 'the right one'—as opposed to sleeping around."[9]

The new traditionalism leads Bridgers to hold romantic views of love and marriage and making home life a priority. Though they want to find a life partner and stick with that person, they are more tolerant than their grandparents. Cross-cultural and interracial unions are not taboo but in fashion. Bridgers may like tradition, but they are not traditional.

Superfragmented

In contrast to the Boomers, who are a homogeneous generation, Bridgers are extremely heterogeneous. Their superfragmentation is observable in their magazines and music.

Magazines fighting for the attention of this generation are adapting by offering numerous subcategories of magazines. For years young girls read *Seventeen, Teen,* and *YM.* Now new entries include *Jump, CosmoGIRL!,* and *Latingirl* that cater to various subgroups. Young men continue to read *Sports Illustrated,* but e-magazines, like *GamePro* and *Nintendo Power,* target different segments of the generation. Still other subcategories include *Transworld Skateboarding* for skateboarders and *Warp* for snowboarders.

As noted previously, the styles of music that attract the attention of Bridgers are highly segmented. The various types of music available divide loyalties so much that no standard style bonds the generation together, as music has tended to do in the past.

Sophisticated

The youngest of the Bridgers, those under twelve years old, are growing up faster than even the Buster generation. Not long ago, children preferred playing with Barbie dolls, climbing trees, or reading about Cinderella. Now, many favor surfing the web, watching teenage movies, or shopping at the mall. Bruce Stein, Mattel's president, acknowledges, "We're losing them sooner. They're in sensory overload. . . . There are so many things competing for their interest."[10]

Bridgers are considered mature at a much younger age than we've seen before. For example, since 1994, Liberty Financial Companies has been pitching mutual funds to children under twelve years old.

What seems to be driving this newfound sophistication is dual-career parents who are practicing a new style of parenting. This new type of parenting gives children more choices about everything. And when young children are given power, they begin to act like adolescents.

Interactive

Bridgers think, organize, and process ideas differently than their elders. They interact with everything around them and appear to have short attention spans as they click from one bit of information to another.

Bridgers use the Internet for communication and research (projects in schools now often require research on the Internet). They use instant messaging and chat rooms. Bridgers watch MTV on their computers and chat with six or seven friends on the Internet at the same time. Parents realize that Bridgers need lots of technical stuff they never had and feel like they are cutting their children off socially if they do not provide technical gadgets.

Bridgers believe the Internet should be free and that no charges should apply to anything that is shared over the Internet. They perceive the recent court decisions that require Napster to charge as unfair.

Demanding

The highly scheduled lifestyle of this generation has left little room for individual thinking or planning. This sequencing of Millennials' schedules creates quick boredom, as well as a loss of creativity, leadership skills, people skills, and conflict-management skills. Bridgers demand to have their time filled with activities.

Those used to high-speed Internet access at college or work find it difficult to work from home on dial-up modems that they consider extremely slow. Young people, who normally talk to friends on-line, leave their computers on all night to receive messages from friends and download music and movies. They find it nearly impossible to use modems that are one hundred times slower than high-speed access. Bridgers expect high performance from technology and are frustrated when it disappoints. A new generation gap—a technology gap—is developing between Bridgers and the generations before them. Their desire for faster access to the Internet carries over into other aspects of life where they demand service and quick response to their needs.

Diverse and Tolerant

As we have seen, Bridgers are the most diverse generation in United States history. More than one-third are minorities. Overall, 82 percent of the Builders are non-Hispanic white. Among Boomers, 75 percent are non-Hispanic white. The Busters are about 69 percent non-Hispanic white and the Bridgers 67 percent.

Having grown familiar with diversity, most Bridgers respect other people and their points of view. They believe it is important to be sensitive to other people's feelings and to avoid hurting them. Therefore, they will listen to what another person believes without challenging him or her. It may be right for you, and that is cool, but it may not be right for me, which is also cool.

Wanting to Be Connected

In the twenty-first century, the phrase "we're all connected" is not just a part of a telephone jingle. The urge to connect is particularly evident among those who embrace technology.

Increasingly Bridgers are turning to the web for a sense of community, as well as for general information. IM—instant messaging—has become a worldwide Bridger phenomenon. This communication tool allows persons to communicate in real time over the Internet even though they are miles apart. According to a report in *Red Herring* in November 2001, 74 percent of Bridgers use IM several times a week, compared to only 44 percent of on-line adults. In addition Bridgers have become almost totally dependent on the Internet to complete their studies. A whopping 94 percent say they use the Internet to complete research papers.[11] They are heavy communicators with access to the Internet, cell phones, and Palm Pilots.

Approximately 5.6 million people used the web in 1994, but that number has risen to at least 50 million in 2001. In 1997 the typical Internet user was a thirty-three year old, affluent, and well-educated male. Among all Internet users in 1997:

5 percent were Builders
42 percent were Boomers
44 percent were Busters
9 percent were Bridgers

While Bridgers do not make up the largest number of Internet users, their usage is growing. As they age and are able to afford computers on their own, it is predicted that they will overtake the other generations in their use of the Internet. They have no fear of technology and quickly learn how to get around on a computer. For them the Internet is a rich resource for new friends, support in time of need, and practical information.

Bridgers believe they couldn't get by without a cell phone, and 35 percent of those twelve to nineteen years old in 2000 own their own cell phone. This figure is projected to be 68 percent by 2005. They use the cell phone as "land line displacement"; they are not tied to a phone that needs to be connected by a land line. Older generations see the phone as a tool, but Bridgers think of a phone as a person, a friend.

Group Reliant

When Boomers were children, friends would ask them, "What does your dad do for a living?" When the older cohort of the Bridgers was growing up, friends asked, "Does your dad live with you?" As the question asked among this generation suggests, many Bridgers lack a nuclear family. In most generations, the peer group weighs heavily in the decisions of young people, and this is particularly true for Bridgers who, because of their circumstances, have learned to be group reliant.

Bridgers trust only those who hang with them 24/7. It is not that they do not trust people over thirty, but that they trust only those they get to know at a deep level. The group they hang with becomes their guide during this portion of their lives. They are resigned to the fact that everyone is flawed in some manner, and they tolerate each other's inadequacies, believing that everyone has problems and not hiding them is a sign of authenticity.

Conclusion

Bridgers are the second largest generation in United States history. As such, it is only a matter of time until they begin to push their agenda and values in the adult world. During the coming fifteen to twenty years, they will begin proposing a new way of thinking in the workplace, homes, and churches of America. By the year 2040 they will begin the process of taking control from the Busters. Church leaders must begin now to understand this newest generation, if they hope to faithfully reach them for Christ in the coming decades.

Bridgers and the Church   11

I f you are not already feeling older after reading the last chapter on the Bridger generation, the following will surely age you. In 2002 the oldest of the Bridger generation is just entering college and the following is a characterization of them as developed by the staff at Beloit College in Wisconsin.

- Bridgers have no meaningful recollection of the Reagan era and probably do not know he was ever shot.
- Bridgers were less than twelve years old when the Soviet Union broke apart, and they do not remember the Cold War.
- Bridgers think bottle caps have always been screw-off and plastic.
- Bridgers are too young to remember the space shuttle blowing up.
- Bridgers have never feared a nuclear war.
- Bridgers do not understand the expression, "You sound like a broken record."
- Bridgers have never owned a record player.

- Bridgers have never seen a black-and-white television or one with only thirteen channels.
- Bridgers have never known anything but in-line roller skates.
- Bridgers have seen only Jay Leno as the host of the *Tonight Show.*
- Bridgers never saw Larry Bird or Magic Johnson play basketball.
- Bridgers think of the Vietnam War as history similar to the Civil War, WWI, and WWII.
- Bridgers have never heard "Where's the beef?" or "I'd walk a mile for a Camel" or "De plane, de plane."
- Bridgers do not have a clue how to use a typewriter.
- Bridgers think MTV has always existed.
- Bridgers do not care who J.R. is or who shot him.
- Bridgers have no idea who Mork was or where he came from.
- Bridgers do not know that Americans were ever held hostage in Iran.
- Bridgers have always cooked popcorn in a microwave.
- Bridgers do not remember Atari, Pong, or Pac Man.
- Bridgers have always had VCRs, cable, answering machines, and CDs.[1]

Ministry to Bridgers

Similar to other generations, a nineteen-year generational span creates two halves, or cohorts, in the Bridger generation. Being the oldest half, the GenYs have been the subjects of most of the research. Study of the younger Millennials is just beginning to take place. Thus most of what we know about this emerging generation is based on the older half. Recognizing that this entire generation is still in their formative years means that prescribing ministry for them should be done carefully.

Postmodern Bridgers are often seen as hip, aloof, demanding, unreachable, searching, and gadget-savvy. They will mature and change in the years to come. However, at this point in the development of Bridgers, church leaders are wise to do the following.

Assist Bridgers to Discover Truth

As a spiritual generation, Bridgers are moving from the generic to the specific and looking for a faith that is rooted in doctrine. Phyllis Tickle, who tracks religious publishing trends for *Publisher's Weekly,* writes about one Bridger who said, "Don't tell me why being a Methodist is better than being a Presbyterian. . . . I'm not going to listen to that . . . but do tell me what it meant originally to be a Methodist. Don't tell me all about spirituality; just tell me what you mean when you say Christian spirituality . . . and then let me decide for myself what to believe."[2]

Churches must help Bridgers discover answers for themselves, rather than simply telling them what to believe. However, Bridgers do need to be taught that truth exists and that challenging other people's viewpoints is okay. In their desire to accept others and their beliefs, Bridgers often overlook the truth of God's written Word.

Give Bridgers Take-Home Value

Growing up in a consumer society has created a highly opinionated consumer generation whose habits will shape the United States for most of the twenty-first century. Bridgers are pragmatic, convenience-focused, and value-insistent when it comes to spending their money or investing their time. What attracts them to an Internet site, a class, or a meeting is its perceived usefulness. Bridgers look for up-to-date content with good service.

To effectively minister to Bridgers, churches must develop practical programs that offer Bridgers immediate take-home value. This generation must be able to see that a given ministry has immediate value for their lives.

Let Bridgers See Your Faith

With AIDS, crime, violence, and divorce casting shadows over their formative years, Bridgers have already faced serious problems. Those who have working parents or single parents have had to assume adult responsibilities early in their lives. This has caused many Bridgers to be more confident, competent, and cautious than other generations at the same age. They are creative, ingenious, and self-actualized. And they do everything their way.

Being cautious, they do not accept statements made by churches at face value but need time to observe church leaders to see if their behavior matches their pronouncements. Wise church leaders will give Bridgers time and space to observe the active faith of church members. Only after seeing the truth lived out in real lives will most Bridgers choose to unite with a community of faith.

Disciple Bridgers Holistically

Bridgers see spiritual growth as a multilayered pilgrimage for one's entire life, rather than a single event or moment in time. Discipling postmodern Bridgers is not about debate, proposition, and linear thought; postmodern discipling is about connection, holism, and dialogue.

In the second half of the last century, many churches made the mistake of separating evangelism and discipleship. This led to the separation of salvation and maturation, the separation of being a believer and being a follower, which was never intended. The Great Commission involves all aspects of salvation, assimilation, and maturation.

This is especially important when it comes to Bridgers, who understand that spirituality involves holistic living. Thus churches must help these young people understand that believing in Christ involves following Christ in all areas of their lives.

Holistic discipleship means leading Bridgers to be followers of Christ from the beginning.

Involve Bridgers Technologically

The generation gap that existed between the Builders and Boomers seems to have disappeared. Forty years ago, parents and kids were arguing over the war in Vietnam, music styles, and commitment levels. The clash between Builders and Boomers was due in part to the difference in educational attainment.

Today the similarities between parents and children are more striking than the differences. According to the Census Bureau, about one-fourth of Boomers and Busters graduated from college and the same percentage is expected of the Bridger generation. Entire families now dress in blue jeans, T-shirts, and sneakers. Most Bridgers respect their parents' opinions and think parents are pretty much up-to-date.

The gap today seems to be a technology gap. Bridgers adapt to technology with greater ease than their parents and grandparents. However, the lack of technological knowledge of older generations is more amusing to Bridgers than a problem.

Churches that desire to attract and keep Bridgers must embrace technology as a ministry tool. Computers and cell phones are necessities in the Bridgers' world, and they assume pastors and churches will use them. They expect churches to use Power Point projection and video clips in worship services, as well as in classes, and they view overhead projectors as old-fashioned. Churches that are serious about ministry to Bridgers will make haste to replace overhead projectors with computer projection systems. Technology must be woven into the fabric of ministry.

Show Bridgers Biblical Tolerance

If we had to choose one word to describe the Bridger generation, it would be *diverse*. As the most ethnically diverse generation to come along, they are the first ones to seriously question traditional racial and ethnic categories. This seems to be due to the fact that they are the first generation not to experience the rigid categories of racism. Many Bridgers are children of mixed races. The largest group are children of black and white parents, but children of white and Asian parents are close behind in numbers. About one in thirty-five Bridgers are of mixed race.[3]

Builders and Boomers were born into a segregated society, with schools, neighborhoods, and public facilities often separated by race or ethnic heritage. The move toward a more integrated society began with the Boomers but has taken off with the Bridgers. Having friends from different racial and ethnic backgrounds, most Bridgers appreciate ethnic foods and have heroes, especially in sports, who are of every race. Bridgers of all backgrounds listen to rap, hip hop, country, and Tejano music.

Bridgers expect churches to be racially and ethnically inclusive. While most churches have had good intentions about being multiracial and multiethnic, in practice it has been exceptionally difficult to build such a church. The Bridger generation may be the one in which multiethnic churches will become a reality.

However, as might be expected, greater racial and ethnic diversity is also creating a polarization among some members of this generation. Hate groups are increasingly visible, most neighborhoods remain segregated, and racial tension among students is still reported. But, even with this backlash, more Bridgers have firsthand experience with integration than any previous generation.

The greater tolerance for diversity in all forms shows up in the Bridgers' acceptance of gays in society. One of the common themes of discussion among Bridgers is homosexuality and bisexuality. While churches must hold to biblical moral and ethical standards, they must demonstrate love for the sinner while hating the sin. And, rather than shying away from such subjects, churches must begin to address these and similar topics with grace.

Help Bridgers Build Strong Families

As the children of divorce, Bridgers are determined to build strong families. Nearly 16 percent of Bridgers grew up with a stepparent. Thus they will likely take longer to choose a mate and take vows of marriage. They desire to be connected to people who are like family to them, which is part of the reason they hunger for the interlinking provided by the Internet, cell phones, and other similar technologies.

Churches have always been strong in promoting marriage and family and this will be an avenue to pursue in reaching Bridgers in the early part of the twenty-first century. In addition, churches must help connect Bridgers with real live local Christians. The dark side of the technology that Bridgers love is that it isolates them from face-to-face relationships and biblical community. One of the challenges of church ministry will be to incarnate the message of Christian community using technology.

Include Bridger Women

Bridger women outnumber Bridger men at college, and by 2020 half of all graduates of computer science programs are predicted to be women. Most Bridgers, nearly 52 percent, feel that a woman working or serving in a leadership role is okay. This new thinking is a result of the women's movement of the 1970s and 1980s, as well as laws like Title 9 that prohibit sex discrimination in college athletics. Add to that the fact that the United States is home to more than nine million companies owned by women (38 percent of all U.S. companies), and one can see that Bridgers are used to women being in leadership.

While Bridger women desire strong families and wish to be available for their children, they still desire to have their own careers. The continuing design on a career seems to be a direct result of the high divorce rate of their parents and grandparents. Essentially they want a career as a means of protection in case they get divorced too. Churches that tap into the unused potential of Bridger women in appropriate ways will find that Bridgers are attracted to their ministry.

Train Bridgers Interactively

Observant church leaders have noticed a cultural change in the Bridger generation. The ministries that effectively reached previous generations are not connecting with the tech-savvy Bridgers. Churches must learn to design worship and study events that present the gospel via multiple venues. Worship and study of the Scripture must be interactive, allowing for those in attendance to collaborate on ideas, insights, and issues.

In an effort to build worship services and study times that Bridgers understand, some churches are experimenting with a new version of the old coffeehouse approach. Often called a video café, this new coffeehouse concept has numerous activities going on at the same time. Bridgers sit around tables talking with their friends while a nearby video projects on a wall or screen. Music from the video or a live band fills the air. Some surf the Internet or talk on cell phones to friends in distant places or just across the room. Candles or dim lights create atmosphere. Leaders or mentors are nearby, available to talk if needed, but not intruding in the conversations unless invited. While such video cafés are not likely to replace worship services, they do appear to be one approach that is reaching Bridgers today.

Conclusion

Bridgers desire to see faith at work in the lives of their leaders and mentors. As churches begin to understand them and develop new approaches to communicate with them, they are open to respond. Faithful churches in the first years of the twenty-first century will redefine the boundaries of technology and help Bridgers become followers of Christ in an interactive way.

Winning
Bridgers

12

No one who has answered the call to help fulfill the Great Commission can ignore the Bridgers. They are open to the gospel, but, as Ron Hutchcraft, president of Ron Hutchcraft Ministries notes, ". . . the 'millennial generation,' so different from the generation that went before, will largely not respond to the traditional outreach approaches with which we are comfortable."[1]

Reaching the Bridger generation with the gospel of Jesus Christ may be the single greatest challenge facing the church today. According to the research by Dr. Thom S. Rainer noted earlier, only 4 percent of them claim to know Jesus Christ as their personal Savior. Depending on whom you read, the consensus is that about 85 percent of people who accept Christ as their personal Savior do so before their twentieth birthday. The Bridgers are our young people, at the age when belief is easiest. If we do not win them to Christ before they become young adults, they may live the rest of their lives without him.

Speaking the Bridger Language

The following insights are not the final answer to the dilemma of reaching Bridgers, but they are some ideas that may spark your creativity.

Create an Environment That Attracts

A primary objective of every ministry to Bridgers should be to create an environment that will attract them. For the most part, this means developing a unique setting where Bridgers can experience spiritual growth in a nontraditional setting. Such a setting must enhance social connections and offer multiple interactive activities. It must be safe and appealing so Bridgers will desire to "hang" with friends there.

As an example, First Church of God in East Central Indiana created a setting called The Living Room. Bridgers find here live music, good food, gourmet coffee, and a smoke-free and alcohol-free atmosphere. It is a warm and welcoming place where Bridgers can engage mentors and peers. The Living Room is located in a converted second-story space in the heart of downtown Muncie next to Ball State.

Similar approaches are being used successfully by other churches. At College Avenue Baptist Church in San Diego, dim lights, candles, and an outdoor coffeehouse welcome Bridgers to The Flood. Community Church of Joy in Glendale, Arizona, started The Crossing. It is a multidimensional effort with a sports and fitness center, classrooms, lounges, arts and learning center, café, and nightclub. Bridgers who attend The Crossing become involved in drama, media productions, technology, a hot line, crisis counseling, and support groups.

Churches throughout the United States are experimenting with other approaches geared to the Bridger lifestyle. Suggested names for such meetings range from Graceland to Boogie Bookstore to ChurchWorks Station.

Share Compelling Stories

Bridgers reject simple formulas and solutions. The simple salvation formulas used in the past, such as the Roman Road, The Four Spiritual Laws, and The Bridge to Life are not as effective as they once were in winning younger people to Christ. Bridgers are not looking for a "Bible answer man" approach to learning but prefer an interactive, multilayered approach whereby they share in the conversation. The key to winning them is to engage them with a compelling true story of faith. We used to call these compelling stories testimonies: A person with a story to tell talks to another person who has a story to tell and shares the story of Jesus in the process. Such a story-telling approach takes more time, as well as good listening skills, but it works when Bridgers are drawn into the process by letting them tell their story and then relating Jesus' story to theirs. The twenty-first century will find Bridgers searching for meaning, which they will find in stories that tell them who they are. Stories have the ability to touch their hearts.

Accept Them into Your Community

What is out is an institutional approach to ministry. What is in is community. In the modern world of the past century, people became involved in communities of faith (churches) after they gave their lives to Christ. It was expected that a person would first believe, then behave or change his or her lifestyle, then that person could belong to the community of faith. In the postmodern world of the twenty-first century, Bridgers want to be involved in community before they give their lives to Christ. The new expectation is that people will first be accepted into the community of faith and there experience and learn about the Christian faith. Then, in the process of belonging, they will come to a point of belief and finally learn to behave. Of course, each church must reach its own comfort level concerning the participation of prebelieving Bridgers. But whatever the determination by a church, it is crucial that Bridgers feel they are accepted as people. We don't have to accept their sin to love and accept them.

Practice Intrigue

Bridgers want to feel like they are ahead of the crowd, decoding something that no one knows about yet. The blatant and obvious mean nothing to them. They are intrigued by the new and cutting edge. For example, in teaching, try using intrigue by telling a Bible story and leaving the ending open. Then let Bridgers decide on their own ending in small discussion groups. After they have had an opportunity to share their endings, then tell the rest of the story by bringing back in the biblical ending. Allow questioning and do not expect passive acceptance. Bridgers are more likely to question authority. They desire to take active roles in designing their own learning events. Ministries that successfully reach Bridgers will welcome questioning and encourage participation.

Become Part of Their Headset

Churches should be involved in establishing relationships with Bridgers even if they are not ready to accept Christ or attend church. Whether Bridgers will become regular churchgoers is anyone's guess, but churches need to close the gap by becoming part of Bridgers' headset.

The problem is figuring out how to get in on the conversation. While the web is one way to communicate with Bridgers, the best way remains face-to-face conversation. As an enthusiastic Bridger shares with another Bridger his or her excitement about Christ and the church, the unchurched Bridger will listen. Personal witness by Bridgers who are committed Christians is key.

Another way to tap into the Bridgers' headset is to take a cue from the business world, which is using the insights of Bridgers to help them decide on products and marketing. Churches can call on Bridgers to help build church web sites, run computer projection equipment, create videos, and develop CDs for teaching and education.

Use On-line Games and Contests

If the 1970s was the "me" decade, the 2000s will be the "linked" decade. Bridgers are increasingly turning to the web for a sense of community and commerce. They use the Internet to socialize and search, to shop and sell. To attract their attention, churches should build a web site that delivers something special.

Developing an interesting web site is a good way to appeal to Bridgers. Web sites that use on-line games and contests are likely to capture their short attention spans. The "click rate" for Bridgers twelve to seventeen years old is 0.19 percent. In other words, they do not stay at a site very long. Thus it takes something unique on a site to get them to stay long enough to read it. They respond best to web sites that offer something for free or practical information.

Use the Radio

Direct mail proved to be an effective way to reach Boomers. However, radio and cable TV advertising may be among the best ways to reach Bridgers. About 95 percent of Bridgers listen to the radio, averaging more than ten hours per week. Radio goes with Bridgers wherever they venture—at home, in their cars, actually wherever they go. Listening to music on the radio, Bridgers can be highly selective and tune into their favorite styles. Radio advertising allows a targeted approach for reaching different segments of the Bridger generation. Segments can easily be selected according to ethnic, gender, and geographical characteristics.

Hang Out 24/7

One thing Bridgers desire is hanging out 24/7. Why do they want this? As we've already seen, relationships are important to Bridgers, and an authentic Christian life will speak louder to them than any Bible study. Careful interpretation of the Bible is important, but Bridgers won't sit through this if a relationship hasn't already been established.

The key is to "hang, hang, hang" by providing lots of ways to interact and participate in activities together. Those who have successfully reached Bridgers spend as much informal time with them as possible, and this should be the mandate of pastoral staff hired to minister directly to Bridgers. When Bridgers can observe truth lived out in real life, they will accept it. "If it's real, it must be true" is one way Bridgers seem to perceive life.

Become Their Mentors

A caring adult can easily influence Bridgers. Studies made of youth from troubled homes who later made good in life have found that in almost all cases a caring adult figure was present as a constant in that kid's life. Divorce-care workshops, discussion groups, counseling programs, retreats, and support groups for children of alcoholics, children from abusive homes, and children living in blended families, all facilitated by a loving adult, will reach the hearts of many Bridgers. Bridgers need parentlike mentors not Bible Study leaders. The key is to understand that Bridgers are not looking for mentors out of weakness but from a sense of loss and hope for the future.

Build on Adrenaline

Going to extremes is one way to characterize Bridgers. According to American Sports Data, Inc., the five fastest growing sports in the United States are, in order of popularity, wakeboarding, snowmobiling, artificial wall climbing, surfing, and paintball. The sports that are declining slightly are cycling, archery, baseball, racquetball, and beach volleyball. Churches that are serious about reaching Bridgers should consider developing events and activities built around these growing sports.

Be Honest and Open

Stick to your core identity. Do not try to be something you are not. Bridgers are astute enough to see through a church and church leaders who do not honestly believe what they are saying. Pastors and other leaders should be themselves and speak directly from their own life experience. One's own personal story of faith is the most powerful message to be delivered to this generation. Being authentic about one's struggles, doubts, and confusion regarding spirituality will get attention and respect.

Engage Their Senses

Technology fosters active learning, and this is all Bridgers know. Delivering truth only through proposition is out. Delivering truth through all the senses is in. Churches that successfully reach Bridgers use interactive approaches rather than passive ones.

Do not expect Bridgers to respond to typical brochures, newsletters, or sermons. Use art, music, poetry, media, the Internet, drama, and lots of stories. Visuals, audio clips, sound bites, and other learning aids are important means of reaching Bridgers.

Conclusion

The Bridger generation may be the greatest challenge for the church in the twenty-first century. But they also may present the greatest opportunity for reaching the world of the twenty-first century for Christ. Bridgers will influence society well into the second half of the new millennium—to at least 2070. As we grow in our understanding of them, we will find new and effective ways of reaching them for Jesus Christ.

> We will not hide these truths from our children
> > but will tell the next generation about the glorious deeds of
> > the Lord.
> We will tell of his power and the mighty miracles he did.

> Psalm 78:4 NLT

The Bridger Generation

Aliases	Generation E (entrepreneurs)
	Ritalin generation
	Mosaics
	NetGen (Internet generation)
	Smorgasbord generation
	Echo Boomerang
	Always-On generation
	Generation Y
	Generation 9-11
	Millennials
Formative Years	1990s, 2000s, and 2010s
Formative Experiences	Postmodern Era
	Technology/Internet
	Variety of music
	MTV
	Diversity
	Columbine High School shootings
	Longer life span
	Speed is king
	Terrorist attacks
	Customized lifestyles
Characteristics	Entrepreneurial
	Tech savvy
	Neotraditional
	Superfragmented
	Sophisticated
	Interactive
	Demanding
	Diverse and tolerant
	Wanting to be connected
	Group reliant
Religious Characteristics	Committed to the group
	Desire interactivity
	Want honest relationships
	Want faith that is authentic
Bridger Ministry	Time to discover truth
	Take-home value
	Model authentic faith
	Holistic discipleship

Use technology
Biblical tolerance and acceptance
Build strong families
Include women
Train interactively

Common Needs and Interests   Desire for authentic faith
Freedom from boredom
Acceptance of others
Techno gadgets
Honest and open talk

Reaching Unchurched Bridgers   Create an environment that attracts
Share compelling stories
Accept them into community
Practice intrigue
Use on-line games and contests
Use the radio
Hang out 24/7
Become their mentors
Build on adrenaline
Be honest and open
Engage their senses

Part 5

Riding the Waves of Change

Reading the Waves   13

S urfers paddle far out into the ocean and patiently wait for just the right wave. Years of experience have taught them that all waves are not equal. Occasionally it appears that a wave is developing, but then it never materializes. Some waves develop but are too small to ride. Many an inexperienced surfer tries to get up on his board and finds that the chosen wave is just too small to provide the needed energy. But surfers who are the most experienced soon learn to read the waves so they can select the best ones to ride.

Riding the generational waves of change requires that we learn how to read the generational waves.

The Generational Theme

The concept of generations is actually quite old, having been a part of human experience for thousands of years. The Bible uses the words *generation* and *generations* 201 times. There are lists of entire families, such as found in Genesis 5. "This is the book of the generations of Adam" (v. 1). And in 6:9: "These are the records of the generations of Noah." There are references to punishment being served on people to the fourth generation (see Exod. 20:5). And Christ references a generational triad when expounding on the resurrection in Matthew 22:32. "I AM THE GOD OF ABRAHAM, AND THE GOD OF ISAAC, AND THE GOD OF JACOB." References are made to an evil generation (Deut. 1:35) and a righteous generation (Ps. 14:5).

It is implied that individuals have responsibility to serve their own generation. In his message to the Antiochians, Paul refers to David's service to his own generation in Acts 13:36: "For David, after he had served the purpose of God in his own generation, fell asleep." There is also a responsibility to teach the next generations (see Ps. 48:13).

Of course, each generation has an evangelistic mandate to communicate the good news to all generations. Psalm 145:4 confirms, "One generation shall praise Thy works to another, and shall declare Thy mighty acts."

Scripture obviously takes the theme of generations seriously. It affirms the different nature of generations, particularly that some generations are more responsive to the gospel than others. What is more, the Bible affirms that there is a natural succession of generations: "A generation goes and a generation comes, but the earth remains forever" (Eccles. 1:4). A similar theme is noted by Homer who compares generations to leaves.

> As the leaves
> of the trees are born and perish,
> thus pass the ages of man:
> old leaves to earth are dashed
> by autumn winds; others nurtured
> by the flowering forest, proudly
> grow in Spring's living breadth;
> and the generations of man are so:
> one is born and another passes away. [1]

Life Span of Generations

The border between two generations is often hard to pinpoint, because a generation exists mostly in the minds of the people who belong to it. When we think of ourselves as part of a generation, studies have found that we usually define ourselves within a fifteen-to-twenty-year range. For example, we usually think of those who were born about the same time as we were as "our" generation. The years that span "our" generation are normally not shorter than fifteen years nor longer than twenty. Thus today we find four major generations: Builders, Boomers, Busters, and Bridgers.

The Builder generation is comprised of three groups—G.I.s, Silents, and War Babies. Due to the slower pace of life, as well as the major formative events of the time, they developed a similar perspective on life. Thus they are viewed as a single generational whole. The three succeeding generations each fit the normal fifteen-to-twenty-year generational span.

Determining a generation, however, involves more than simply the span of years. The formative events must also come together to develop a generational mindset. The clearest example of a generation that has both the required span of years and unified consciousness is the Boomers. All researchers are in basic agreement that the Boomer generation began in 1946 and ended in 1964. Disagreement arises when attempting to designate the Busters and Bridgers. The Busters are a true "bust" generation if they are defined by the years 1965 to 1976. The problem comes when we realize that eleven years is short of the normal fifteen to twenty years needed to define a generation. Using the years 1965 to 1983 makes more sense, especially when looking at the events that formed them. Likewise, using the years 1984 to 2002 for the Bridgers best fits the normal pattern of generations.

Overlap of Generations

There is, of course, a great deal of overlap at the edges of the generations. This is especially true with the Busters and Bridgers, which explains why some want to include the youngest Busters in the Bridger generation. For example, Susan Mitchell, an authority on generational studies, paints a demographic picture of persons eighteen to thirty-four years old as Generation X (the Busters).[2] Yet a sister publication calls those seven to twenty-four years old Millennials (the Bridgers).[3] Clearly, there is an overlap between these two generations that makes it difficult to determine precisely when one begins and the other ends.

As one can see in the illustration below, some overlap between generations took place between Builders and Boomers, even more between Boomers and Busters, but a great deal of overlap occurs between Busters and Bridgers.

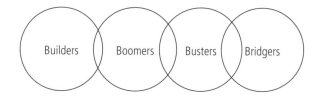

Succession of Generations

Clearly there has always been a succession of generations. In times when there has been a short life span, there have normally been only three generations alive at one time. Yet in times of a longer life span, four or more generations typically interact together. Thus, at the beginning of the 1900s, when life expectancy was under fifty years, only three generations were interacting together in most situations. As we enter the twenty-first century, life expectancy is approaching eighty years, which means at least four, and perhaps five, generations are interacting together.

The struggle that has taken place in the last fifty years between generations is due in part to the intersection of two major trends: longer lives and rapid change. The pace of change has created a "generation gap" and "technology gap" in knowledge and experience. Longer lives have meant more generations are interacting together; they each push their own views and agendas. In such an environment, it is not surprising that there are conflicts and misunderstandings between generations.

Understanding the natural succession of generations in terms of their influence is important. We have described these generations as young, adult, mature, and senior. Historically the young generation is *preparing* to contribute to society as adults; they are studying, learning, and experiencing life. The Bridgers are filling this generational role today. The adult generation is *promoting* their view of the world and life. The Busters are now in this phase and, although they are not in control of much, they are beginning to make headway in influencing life with their perspectives. Today's mature generation is the Boomers. They are *prevailing* in the sense that it is their worldview that predominates in society, business, and life. The senior generation is, of course, the Builders who are exiting the arena of life, literally and, as far as their influence is concerned, are now *informing* the younger generation from their past experience and wisdom.

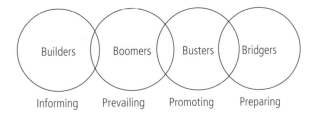

It is this natural progression of preparing, promoting, prevailing, and informing that creates the tension between generations. When the events of life are not dramatic or the pace of change is slow, the tension created in the succession of generations is mild. However, in times of rapid and climactic change, the generational progression creates lots of frustration and conflict, which is what has been taking place during the past half century.

Undercurrents of Discontent

As leaders who are trying to navigate through the waves of generational change in our churches, we will find ourselves pulled in several different directions by the undercurrents of discontent among our members. Being aware of where these undercurrents are and understanding a little bit of what causes them will help us ride safely over the waters of change.

Developing a ministry that meets the needs of the four generations may create several disruptive undercurrents. The following are the main ones faced by most churches when the generations collide.

Conflict over Worship Styles

The most visible ministry in which generational conflict shows up is the worship service. Disagreements over worship are so common that some pastors jokingly note that when Satan fell from heaven, he landed in the choir loft and has been making trouble in the music and worship service of the church ever since.

While not every member of each generation sees things the same way, essentially the areas of difficulty are as follows:

- *Pace of the service.* Builders like worship services to move along slowly and predictably. Boomers like worship to move at a fast clip, while Busters and Bridgers want it to move even quicker. Both Busters and Bridgers look for variety and spontaneity.
- *Brightness of the lighting.* Builders prefer softer lighting as it gives more of a worshipful feeling. Boomers look for a

brighter lighting so they can see people well. Most Busters and Bridgers also like brighter lighting, but some prefer a darker setting, perhaps with candles or other subdued lighting.

- *Loudness of sound.* Builders appreciate being able to hear well but dislike sound that blasts. Boomers and Busters want the music loud enough that they can feel it. Some Bridgers also appreciate louder sound and in some situations are comfortable with lots of interactive noise from videos, music, and talking. There is a trend in some areas of the United States toward acoustical music without the loud amplification.

- *Length of service.* Builders have a longer attention span and thus are willing to sit through longer services. The attention span of Boomers, Busters, and Bridgers has been increasingly shorter. It is difficult to make a sweeping statement regarding preferred length of time for worship. In most situations there is still a preference for a service that is no longer than seventy-five minutes. Yet some Busters and Bridgers appreciate a longer worship service with up to an hour of music and an hour for the message.

- *Formality of service.* Builders expect a certain level of formality and decorum, whereas Boomers prefer somewhat of a dressy casual. Busters and Bridgers like things to be flexible and casual. Builders equate reverence with formality of dress. They experience great frustration with Bridgers who may wear baseball caps in the church, perhaps even while in the worship service.

- *Feel of the service.* Builders look for a worship service that is quiet and reverent. Boomers and Busters desire an upbeat celebration time. Bridgers, however, appear to appreciate worship that is real and honest regardless of the style.

- *Participation in the service.* Builders tend to watch and enjoy while Boomers and older Busters who grew up in church like to participate with clapping and similar forms of involvement. Bridgers like a highly interactive worship service that allows for multiple forms of involvement. Unchurched Boomers, Busters, and Bridgers want to be entertained to some extent.

- *Type of music.* Builders love the hymnal and the familiar songs of the faith. They like their music to be slowly paced and reverent. Boomers appreciate the praise music of the '70s and '80s, while Busters and Bridgers like to "sing a new song" to the Lord using a variety of music styles.

- *Quality.* Builders associate quality with the effort that is extended. Thus a person may sing off-key, but Builders appreciate the quality of his or her effort. Boomers see quality as being mistake free. They expect the music, sound, announcements, and message to be well done. Busters and Bridgers tend to view quality as equal to authenticity. To them a Boomer worship service comes across as too slick and contrived. A few mistakes in the worship service are fine with them, as it is more authentic and real.

Clash over Sermon Form

Sermons may be characterized as either vertical or horizontal. Vertical sermons stress the exposition of the Bible and tend to be oriented to touching people's minds. Builders like to nod in agreement with the truth they already know. They love to hear the old, old story over and over.

Horizontal sermons stress the practical application of the Bible and tend to be oriented to touching people's hearts. Boomers, Busters, and Bridgers appreciate the old, old story, but they want to be challenged with what they do not already know. "You touched my heart" is their idea of a good message.

The Builder generation usually likes a traditional message. Some like an in-depth Bible sermon and others prefer a more evangelistic message.

Boomers and Busters usually prefer a message with life application. They long for some practical word that will help them get through the week. As one person put it, "I'm more concerned about getting through Monday morning than how the people of Israel got through the Red Sea." Bridgers desire a message that appears authentic.

The changing nature of generations reflects directly on sermon styles. In a way, the four generations can be viewed as a continuum. On the left (represented by the Builders) are those who believe the primary preaching style should focus on proposition, principles, theories, systematic theology, apologetics, and classic linear thought. In contrast is the right side (represented by the Bridgers), who believe the primary preaching style should focus on biblical and narrative theology, storytelling, and bio- and autobiographical teaching. The left side can be described as more of a New Testament style and the right side as more of an Old Testament style. Narrative and propositional preaching are both biblical forms, but in today's postmodern environment, it appears that it is best to start on the right side and move to the left in terms of style. This explains in part, why topical preaching has risen in popularity during the last quarter century.

Dissension over Bible Translations

Older Builders usually appreciate the formality and beauty of the King James Version of the Bible, although many have switched to newer translations. Boomers, Busters, and Bridgers want to use translations that are written in modern English, which is easier to understand. Often it is difficult for everyone in a church to agree to use one translation, so they all bring their personal favorite. This can be a problem for congregational reading of the Bible. The best solution is to print the Scripture to be read in the program or project it on a screen so everyone has the same version for congregational reading.

Differing Views of the Church

Builders know that the church is really the people and not the building, but in practice they think of the building as God's house, and they can be emotionally attached to the church structure. In many cases it took a lot of sacrifice and money to build the structure, and Builders want to protect it. They may object to coffee in the sanctuary and the youth using the fellowship hall.

Boomers and Busters do not view the church building as sacred in any way. To them the facility is there to be used for ministry. So coffee is allowed in the sanctuary, and it's fine for the children to play Nerfball soccer in the fellowship hall. Bridgers view the church as primarily a place of community; as such they see the building as a resource to be used but not worshiped.

As far as management of the church is concerned, Builders want to know what's going on. They attend business meetings to check up on the pastors and church leaders. Most Boomers, Busters, and Bridgers seem willing to give leaders responsibility and authority and to trust them to act wisely. Builders like to vote on every issue, including what color to paint the church kitchen. Boomers, Busters, and Bridgers are willing to leave such decisions up to the leaders.

Annoyance over Church Attendance

Most Builders were raised during the one-breadwinner system. When the mother did not work outside the home, there was more time for church participation and volunteerism. It was not unusual for the family to spend several evenings a week at church activities. A strong commitment to Christ was and is played out in a strong commitment to church attendance.

Most Boomers, Busters, and Bridgers are part of a dual-income or single-parent family. The pressure of both parents working outside the home leaves much less time to go to church. They will often be too tired to attend church in the evening and will decide to stay home and spend time together. Their strong commitment to Christ is played out in commitment to their relationships and community.

Disagreement over Missions Priorities

Builders have placed a priority on foreign missions. Participation in two world wars convinced Builders that sin was real.

They saw it face-to-face, especially as they freed the death camp survivors in Germany. The growing economy of the 1950s provided the necessary income to support foreign missions, and the general philosophy of ministry developed that a church that supported foreign missions would grow and one that did not would fail.

Boomers found that their efforts to change the world were not very successful. They tried to bring about world peace and to break down racial barriers. To some extent they have seen changes, but many have found that the greatest successes come when working on problems in the local community. Thus they tend to focus on missions close to home.

Busters find it difficult to be involved in a mission by simply giving money toward it. They want to do something, so they become involved in local projects. Boomers and Busters often feel that Builders were wrong to stress foreign missions while neglecting the families and problems in their own neighborhoods.

The Bridgers like to serve together as a faith community. Doing something nice for people at home is better than focusing on people they do not know, but short-term mission trips are an excellent way to get them involved at a broader level.

Struggle over Pastoral Care

Builders see pastoral care as the responsibility of the paid pastoral staff, particularly the senior pastor. Boomers, Busters, and Bridgers want to practice the "one anothers" of Scripture and care for each other.

Builders expect to be visited. Boomers, Busters, and Bridgers are often surprised by and even uncomfortable with a visit. They would rather "do lunch" or "hang out" or meet for breakfast.

Disunity over the Use of Drama and Video

Builders are used to having everything in print, from songs in a hymnal to announcements in the bulletin. They are uncomfortable with information in church being delivered through video and drama.

Boomers are very comfortable with all audiovisual media, which have been a part of their lives for as long as they can remember. Busters and Bridgers are even more attached to computer-generated projections. It seems appropriate to use audiovisuals in church because they can help clarify the message. In particular, Bridgers like a highly interactive environment.

Contention over Programs

Builders experienced the success of traditional programs like the Sunday evening worship service, midweek prayer meeting, and Sunday school. They remember times when these services and programs were the foundation of the church.

Time-pressed Busters and Boomers see some of these traditional programs and services as ineffective time wasters and would like to see them canceled or at least restructured into more effective formats. Bridgers are looking for ministries that allow them freedom of choice to attend what matters to them personally.

Builders are especially nostalgic about the Sunday school. Many remember being taken to Sunday school by their parents. Prior to the 1950s, Sunday schools tended to be evangelistic, and numerous Builders received the Lord as their Savior while attending. Builders are critical of small groups if time is spent only in fellowship and not in Bible study. Many resist the personal sharing so common in small groups.

Most Busters and many Boomers see Sunday school as a boring time primarily geared to children. Since World War II, the goal of most Sunday schools has been education rather than evangelism, and the content-orientation of most Sunday schools today is contrary to what Boomers and Busters are looking for—relationships. They prefer small-group meetings where they can get to know people, open up, share their hurts, and receive support. They do not think the traditional Sunday school can meet those needs.

The Bridgers like both small groups and large groups. Those who lack well-developed people skills feel uncomfortable sharing in a small-group setting and look for large-group meetings to attend where they have freedom to remain quiet and anonymous.

Conclusion

Classical music has been disappearing from the American cultural scene for the past three decades. Belatedly realizing that American culture has changed faster than they have, major American symphony orchestras are contemplating in what form they might endure. "We're fossils, and if we don't change, we'll remain fossils," comments Paul Freeman, American conductor.[4]

For church leaders who find themselves dealing with the problems caused by the collision of changing generations in their churches, the best advice is to be open to change. If we struggle and try to fight our way back to the way things used to be, we will expend a lot of useless energy and may drown in our own efforts. Instead of fighting, we need to relax and go with the flow, seeking to understand what is taking place. Later there will be time to adjust to the flow and develop a model of ministry that is just right for the congregation.

I'm not talking about doctrinal or spiritual compromise. If we get caught in the flow of doctrinal error, we must fight it with all the energy we have. But in reference to the functional changes taking place in our churches, we need to take a wise approach. We should be willing to use whatever methods or models work best, without compromising our message or integrity.

Linking
Generations

14

A n article in the real estate section of a local newspaper highlighted a new home development, which was built for multiple-generation families. Homebuilders and architects have become aware that families are once again living together as multigenerational units. Throughout history it has been common for multigenerational families to live close together, if not actually under the same roof.

After World War II the development of the suburbs and freeways and the resulting mobility of people broke geographic generational ties. Families began to live in small nuclear units rather than in extended family units. Now, as we enter the twenty-first century, families are once again finding it economically advantageous for several generations to pool their resources and live together.

The residences being advertised in the newspaper article were in Las Vegas, but a similar trend is taking place in other metropolitan areas of the United States. The architect who designed the new multigenerational homes for the Las Vegas development says, "Our consumer research for this house shows that today's families require flexible floor plans that accommodate multiple generations." He continues, "We designed [the homes] for a moderately affluent, multigenerational family—a mother, father, two children and live-in grandparent. The home breaks into separate functional areas—shared family spaces as well as private retreats for each generation."[1]

This blending of generations in living arrangements is something that needs to be followed in our church ministries. Some churches today specifically target Boomers or Busters, but for most existing, traditional churches, this kind of narrow focus is not possible. Most pastors and church leaders know that they must work with all generations in the same church without ignoring any of them.

New Approaches

For churches that desire to minister in our changing generational scene, there are six primary models being used today.

The Seeker-Centered Model

Seeker-centered churches are those that target their Sunday ministries almost exclusively to the unchurched, which makes their focus unique. Everything from the facility to the music to the message is designed to make a favorable impression on the unchurched person. It is a complete reversal of the traditional church, which tends to target its facilities, music, and message to the church person. Seeker-centered churches tend to

- have a concern for demographic research
- profile unchurched people
- use a neutral church name
- offer a nontraditional atmosphere
- preach practical messages

The Seeker-Sensitive Model

A close cousin to the seeker-centered model, seeker-sensitive churches include churches that use a worship style that is sensitive to the unchurched but does not exclusively target them. These churches target their ministries primarily to Christians while maintaining sensitivity to unchurched guests. Seeker-sensitive churches tend to

- see worship as evangelism
- welcome guests as one of their own
- give unchurched participants time to observe

The Multiple-Track Model

Multiple-track churches are those that offer distinct approaches to ministry at different times, particularly in two or more worship services. This model of ministry is the reverse of the blended model, which seeks to combine different approaches into one service.

The multiple-track model is quite popular among churches with large contingencies of different generations. It allows the use of distinct philosophies of ministry at the same time. Churches using this model tend to

- offer different styles of worship in separate services
- offer separate ministries for each generation
- allow for lots of diversity
- provide ways for the generations to minister to each other
- reach multiple target groups

The Satellite Model

Churches using the satellite model are those that have one or more worship services in different geographical locations. This model is not as well-known or as popular as the first three due to the logistical difficulties involved in making it work. Churches using this model

- are extremely healthy
- are committed to evangelizing a different generation
- are not afraid to take risks
- have a senior pastor with a long tenure
- have the talent and management skills to pull it off

The Rebirthed Model

Rebirthed churches are those that completely stop using one philosophy of ministry and begin using a new philosophy. There are very few churches using this model in the United States, but many smaller churches should give it serious consideration in the future. Smaller churches that struggle to meet their budget and provide effective ministries might find a rebirth their only hope for renewed life and vitality. Usually churches using this model

- are very small
- face a major loss of attendance, funds, and ministry effectiveness
- have a core of people who have a vision for a new style of church
- have a pastor with the same new vision and, in some cases, a church-planting background
- may have a sense of desperation

The Blended Model

Blended churches are those that combine two or more differing philosophies of ministry, usually in the worship service. Churches using this model are characterized by

- two styles of music in one worship service

- traditional ministries and new ones side-by-side
- changing terminology
- a transitional atmosphere
- continuing tension over the philosophy of ministry

A Closer Look at Blending

Blending is a popular approach used by some churches, attempting to blend the traditional and the contemporary in hopes of pleasing all generations enough so that they remain in the church.

Before discussing blending, we need to return briefly to the general characteristics of the four generations on which this book has focused. We need to clearly understand that the four generational divisions broadly discussed in the first four parts of this book cannot be rigidly applied to a group of people. The figure below illustrates a strict view of the separate generations. Perceived in this manner, we might get the idea that every person in each generation thinks exactly the same. Of course this is not true. The general characteristics of each generation are strictly true of only about three-fourths of each generation.

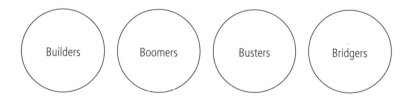

A wise pastor once noted, "There are old young people and young old people." Similarly, there are overlapping attitudes and characteristics among every generation that go beyond age or the particular generation in which an individual is born. Some Boomers will be very traditional in their outlook on church and ministry, while some Builders will enjoy the excitement of contemporary music and worship. The figure below illustrates these overlapping attitudes.

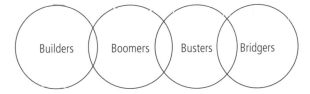

There is overlap of the generations at both ends. Since people born at the beginning or end of each generation grow up during a transition from one generation to another, they feel strong pulls both ways and may go in either direction. It is very common to find some older Boomers who identify more with the Builders than with their own generation. Likewise, there will be some Busters who identify more with Boomers, and the opposite is also true. In many situations Busters and Bridgers will be more alike than different.

We find that relationships between generations are even more complex. There are traditionalists in every generation who may identify with those a generation removed. Builders who once argued with their Boomer children over the Beatles' music may today accept the more aggressive music of their Buster grandchildren. And some Busters may feel very comfortable in their grandparents' church.

What Is Blending?

When church leaders talk about blending, they usually are thinking of the worship service. No other ministry in a church reflects the values and philosophy of a church as clearly or as publicly. Worship is the one ministry in a church where all the members come and participate. The need for blending in other areas of ministry, such as Sunday school, is not as critical since the individual classes allow each generation the opportunity to do ministry in their own unique manner. Blending of musical styles has become, according to researcher John C. LaRue Jr., the primary style of churches in 2001. He reports that 22 percent of churches employ a contemporary style, 35 percent use a traditional style, and 43 percent practice a blended style of worship.[2]

From a technical viewpoint, blending is the combining of two or more differing philosophies of ministry. Usually the differing philosophies involved are called traditional and contemporary.

An attempt at blending in the worship service usually takes one of two forms. In the first, the worship time is segmented into two evenly divided sessions. One session will include music in a traditional style while the other uses music in a contemporary style. One may use the organ and piano with hymns led by a song leader. In the other, a worship leader directs praise songs, accompanied by a small band. Although this option may meet the needs of all worshipers, the service may seem too choppy and fragmented. In addition, the generations tend to participate wholeheartedly only in the style they feel comfortable with, which reduces the volume and dynamic feel so important to a positive worship service.

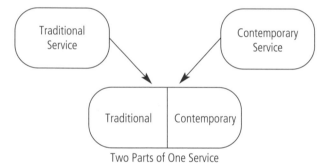

Two Parts of One Service

A second approach to blending attempts to develop an entirely new style for worship, instead of using both traditional and contemporary styles as described above. The usual approach is to soften the contemporary music and speed up the traditional music so that the service becomes acceptably contemporary or blended.

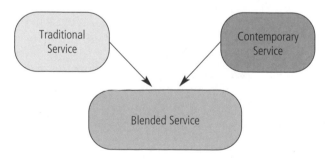

Most churches that wish to blend their worship services find that this second approach works best since it effectively weaves the two styles into a common, unified whole. Developing such a blended church usually takes some time, as illustrated by the following true story.

Faith Community Church was born during the church-planting boom of the early 1950s. Initially there was rapid growth, but following the resignation of the founding pastor, the church plateaued. By its twenty-second anniversary the average member's age was over fifty. During this same period of time the local neighborhood gradually changed, attracting many Boomers due to the affordable housing. Faith found it was a Builder church unable to reach its Boomer community. With the calling of a twenty-nine-year-old pastor, the church began to make some strategic changes to blend the Boomers with the Builders. Over a period of ten years several changes took place resulting in a blended church with members of an average age of less than forty.

In the initial stage of change the large pulpit was replaced with a smaller one. The hard wooden pews were sold and replaced with movable padded chairs. A new hymnal was purchased that contained some contemporary praise songs. Gradually the congregation began to use the sanctuary as a multipurpose room, which allowed for gradual experimentation with different worship styles. For the evening service, the chairs were positioned at a different angle than used in the morning service. Various teaching techniques were tried in the evening, such as interviews, question-and-answer times, and panel discussions. Small groups were established, and new ministries directed to the needs of younger families were started. Today Faith is a totally blended congregation, using primarily a contemporary style of worship and music, with a few traditional elements woven into the worship fabric.

Nine Steps for Blending

The following are vital steps that should be taken by church leaders who desire to blend Builders, Boomers, Busters, and Bridgers into one church.[3]

1. *Get senior pastor's support.* It is often said that what is endorsed from the pulpit will succeed, and what is not will fail. The pastor must play the key role in planning, educating, and leading the church toward a blended ministry. For such a different emphasis to take place, the senior pastor must be committed to it and work to make it happen. No matter how strong the pressure, it is wise never to attempt to build a blended ministry without the senior pastor's full involvement.

Going beyond simple endorsement of the strategy, a pastor must be comfortable with and able to mesh two differing philosophies of ministry into a single new form. If the pastor's ministry has been geared to only one generation, he must be willing to communicate to a blended audience, find and use new illustrations, change his wardrobe (perhaps wearing a sweater and tie on Sunday morning), develop a relational style, adapt his vocabulary to be meaningful to all members, accept criticism, support the musicians and staff both publicly and privately, share creative leadership with a worship team, and patiently give the process time. A blended service that is well done is complex and difficult to do. It takes a lot of planning, and a pastor must be willing to prepare sermons and plan worship services two or three months in advance.

2. *Get support of lay leaders.* Lay leaders in the congregation must be willing to follow the pastor's lead. Their personal and group commitment to disciple making must cause them to see the needs and opportunities available in a blended church. They must team with the pastor in a strategic, long-term plan to bring the generations together.

A solid commitment to outreach and assimilation will undergird their willingness to try a blending approach to worship. Criticism will come from saints who feel that they are being neglected. As this occurs, the leaders' commitment to finding and keeping the lost *one* will need to outweigh the pressure to minister to the *ninety-and-nine* who are already in the church (see Luke 15:4–7).

3. *Help the congregation see the opportunities and needs.* Existing congregations must develop a desire to reach those of other generations; usually it's a congregation of Builders and Boomers

who must reach out to Busters and Bridgers. Church leaders should plan to spend a minimum of six to twelve months creating such a consciousness before many changes or new strategies are implemented. Take the time to build a solid biblical foundation, share the vision for a new style of ministry, listen to people's concerns, adjust the proposed strategy, and pray.

4. *Stress biblical concepts of love and acceptance.* Diversity and variety are two words that characterize the Boomer, Buster, and Bridger generations. The divergent views, desires, and expectations of members of the four generations will require acceptance and love. Sermons, classes, and small groups should focus on these divergent ideas during the blending period. In particular, stress the "one another" commands found in the New Testament and structure opportunities for people from different generations to practice them in small group settings. For example, instruct one another (Rom. 15:14), serve one another (Gal. 5:13), and submit to one another (Eph. 5:21).

5. *Establish an alternate worship service or a new class in which blending can be practiced.* It could be an evening worship service, a Sunday school class, or a small group. If this is not possible, an occasional praise or celebration service where new styles of music can be introduced will gradually introduce the congregation to blending. The gradual approach will help people accept new ideas, which can eventually be introduced on a regular basis.

The model service ought to reflect a balance of traditional and contemporary styles in music, participation, relationships, and dialogue. It works best if the organization, transitions, feel, and flow of the new blended service are well thought out and developed before you go public with the service. The best resource for learning how to do this is other churches that have already traveled this path. Also see chapter 15 for ideas.

6. *Educate the generations so they understand each other.* A common term used in the 1960s to describe the gulf between Builders and Boomers was *generation gap.* Generation gaps had been relatively unknown in earlier times since the slowness of change created very little difference in viewpoints between gen-

erations. The rapid pace of change since 1950 has made generation gaps real.

How each generation views the gap is different. Younger generations tend to focus on the intrinsic differences in values, and older generations tend to focus on the immaturity seen in the personal habits and styles of the younger. Teaching from the pulpit must be geared to help each group see the value of the other. Key areas of concern are music, expression of worship, relational values, institutional values, and commitment levels. Everyone who speaks from the platform should take great care to affirm and hold up each generation. In no case should a generation ever be criticized publicly. The congregation gets its cues from its leaders. What is said and done during the worship service will flow down into the rest of the church.

Meet with Sunday school classes and small groups to teach about the strengths and values of each generation. These smaller forums allow for questions and answers as well as providing a safe place for people to vent their frustrations. By using these smaller forums, you will circumvent the possibility of an explosion of frustration in a larger setting, which may damage the entire body. As needed, meet with individuals over breakfast or lunch to hear their concerns.

In many cases the use of outside speakers or church consultants can prove to be a powerful change motivator. Being from the outside, they have several advantages, such as being able to say things that could not be said by a member of the church family, having a more objective outlook, and being viewed as an expert on the issue.

7. *Foster common-ground experiences.* Generations tend to drift apart in churches. Scheduling classes, small groups, and activities around life stages is a natural process, but it tends to segregate the generations and limit their communication. Offering age-graded activities is proper, and there is no need to blend every ministry in a church. It does help generations to understand and love each other, however, when they spend time together. Leading up to and during the initial stages of developing a blended worship service, it is wise for church leaders to provide common-ground experiences for the generations.

A new-members class could introduce people to the values, goals, and history of all four generations. A parenting class might be attended by a mix of Boomers, Busters, and Builders. The Builders could share the struggles they went through raising young children and answer questions. Since many Busters, in particular, may have come from homes where parenting skills were not well modeled, this could provide a solid opportunity to build bridges between the generations. An effort should be made to make small groups intergenerational. Many Builders, Boomers, and Busters enjoy being around people of the other generations. Of course, as Bridgers begin having children, they should also be added to this class.

8. *Organize a new-members task force.* The responsibility of this task force would be to help new people develop several friends in the church, find a place to serve, and identify a class or group where they would feel comfortable. Representatives from each generation should serve on the task force. It is crucial that the task force include people who are recent newcomers to the church (within one or two years), so they remember what it was like to have been a new member. They can help new people understand and fit into the existing church structure with a minimum of frustration.

9. *Encourage Boomers and Busters to take leadership.* If Builders have been the main leaders of your church, qualified Boomers and Busters must gradually be allowed and encouraged to assume key positions of leadership throughout the church structure. These would include the worship team, new-members committee, the worship committee, the music committee, the small-group committee, the activities (social/sports) committee, as well as regular boards, such as elders, deacons, or trustees. While members of the Bridger generation are still a little young for most leadership positions, they must be used where appropriate, such as on a worship team, teaching children, serving at camps, and so on.

It is crucial that the worship team be intergenerational. The leaders who are seen on the platform influence the people who will attend the service. When people come to a church, one of the first things they do is look around to find people like themselves. The people on the platform communicate a tacit message about who attends the church, so, in a blended worship service, care must be taken to have people of all ages up front. If the members of the worship team on the platform are only from the Builder generation, then the service will naturally attract Builders but not Boomers, Busters, or Bridgers. If a church wishes to attract and hold Busters, then it must have Busters on the platform. If the senior pastor comes from the Builder generation, then it is even more important that Boomers, Busters, and Bridgers be visibly present before the congregation.

Some Cautions

A well-conceived and executed worship service of any type is more difficult to pull off than it looks to most people. And a blended service can be the most difficult of all. Remember that a blended worship service is likely to be a temporary worship form on the journey to a new form that is just right for your congregation. The exact mix or blend of worship elements may change several times on the journey. Blended worship tends to discourage those who want only one type of service. These people may become disheartened and move to other churches that offer what they want. Be aware that blended services may (1) be difficult to lead, (2) result in disruption, and (3) cause a lost sense of direction.

Blending at its best is transitional. In truth, blending is not the destination but the journey, and where worship services end up stylistically may not be known for many years. Some keen observers of churches feel that blending will lead only to a fully contemporary worship service. Others sense that we are in the dynamic process of creating an entirely new form of worship, which will be evident only over time.

Until that new form of worship is developed, blending generational styles in one service has proved a practical way to go. At the least, blending allows a church to

- demonstrate the unity of the church
- meet different needs

- provide diverse ministry opportunities
- honor the past and the future
- give people time to change

Conclusion

Vital, growing churches in the next decade will be those that can successfully reach, win, and keep the Boomer, Buster, and Bridger generations. For this to happen in existing churches, leaders need to make bold, long-term plans for blending Builders, Boomers, Busters, and Bridgers into a unified church. Of course, there are risks involved in attempting a blend, but the call of Christ to make disciples makes the risks worthwhile.

Wave Runners   15

Anyone who has watched people on water skis has observed them crisscrossing and hopping over the wake created by the boat that is pulling them along. Jumping the small wakes created by boats appears to be easily done. Water-skiers seem to master the technique quite easily, and they always seem to have fun doing it.

One of the most popular innovations in water recreation has been the development of Jet Skis or Sea-doos. These small water vehicles allow the driver to sit, kneel, or stand up while he jets around a lake or ocean, much like water skiers but without the necessity of a towing boat. In lakes it is common to see these Jet Skis running easily over the wakes created by boats or other Jet Skis. But in the ocean, where the waves are much larger, it becomes more of a challenge. Still the people running the waves appear to have great fun.

Occasionally one of these wave runners will attempt to jump over a large wave or perhaps try to cross one at a wrong angle. When this happens, the craft often capsizes, throwing the rider off. Fortunately the manufacturers of these water vehicles thought about this and built in a device that causes the Jet Ski to stay in one place and simply move around in circles. This allows the rider time to swim back to the Jet Ski and continue with his fun.

Wave running over the wakes created by changing generations in a local church can be as much fun as running waves in a lake. At other times, it can be disastrous. Sometimes the wakes caused by generational change are fairly small. Other times they are like the overwhelming waves of the ocean. Occasionally they become tidal waves, too powerful for anyone to jump.

As wave runners in our churches, we need to be aware of the generational changes taking place and structure a plan to effectively run the waves of change.

Implications for the Future

We actually know very little about change and what we know is changing, and we can be sure that the future is going to be different from the past. Take television, for instance. Television began in 1939. The battery-powered television came in 1950. In 1956 the first portable black-and-white sets were introduced. NBC began broadcasting all programs in color in 1966. By the early 1980s, 98 percent of all homes in the United States owned at least one TV set, some even more. Today we have HDTV (high-definition television), and some predict that we will soon have hologram televisions where three-dimensional figures act out scenes on our living room floors.

The point is, nothing is staying the same. Times change and so do the generations. Here are a few selected implications for churches as the generational waves flow through them.

The Builder Wave

Studies show that we all think of ourselves as fifteen years younger than we actually are.[1] So members of the Builder generation may be younger, at least in their hearts, than we think.

However, the ability of the Builder generation to carry on programs and projects is waning as they age.

Builders will continue to support the church financially, depending on their disposable income and other factors. As loyal followers, they will certainly continue to give sacrificially, as they always have done. When he was getting ready to build a new church facility, Pastor Doug Murren of Eastside Foursquare Church in Kirkland, Washington, discovered who gives the most money. He writes, "First, I found in preparing to build a new facility that at least 80 percent of funding for Christian organizations comes from people 55 and older."[2] With this in mind, church leaders must begin now to educate Boomers, Busters, and Bridgers about financial stewardship. If we do not, we can surely expect the financial giving to churches to go down.

Revivalistic evangelism styles will continue to decline along with the Builder generation. This style of evangelism rose to popularity during a time when people needed entertainment as well as the Lord. Builders brought their friends to church so that the preacher could win them to Christ. It was a ministry style that worked well at one time but not so well anymore. Now people do not need the church for entertainment, but they still need the Lord. Now evangelism is best done through a friendship approach, rather than a program approach.

Loyalty to institutions will continue to decline along with the Builder generation. The three generations following on the heels of the Builders have not seen much in government, savings and loans, or other institutions to raise their trust level. We will need to win the loyalty of Boomers, Busters, and Bridgers one by one through excellent service and culturally relevant ministry.

The Boomer Wave

As the Boomers continue to take over control of the leadership of existing churches, it is likely that a number of changes will take place. The Boomers support people-oriented programs, and as leaders they will evaluate old ministries against this value. Programs and projects that can show they are honestly making a difference in people's lives are being kept; those that cannot are being discontinued.

Financial stewardship is related to people projects and vision. One thing for sure, Boomers do not give their money to pay bills. They give it to support vision. Boomers can never get away from the '60s when they poured their lives into big concerns like civil rights. Churches that continue to give Boomers a big vision will get their time, their money, and their emotional support. We have the "cause of all causes," but we must learn to communicate it with passion and in the language of today if we want to attract the Boomers' commitment.

Friendship evangelism will continue to be strong for the Boomer generation. Unchurched Boomers will be open to hearing the gospel from their friends, so the sharing of testimonies and the gospel will need to take place within the network of relationships. "Let's do lunch" will be received better than "Come to the men's breakfast on Saturday morning."

Loyalty to people is the prime motivator for Boomers in the church. The ministries that are likely to survive are ones that are built around relationships. Ministries that are casual and flexible and that operate with a simple structure will be popular.

The Buster Wave

It is taking some time, but gradually Busters are helping churches become involved in issue-oriented projects. No other generation has had as much concern for the environment, and as they have opportunity, they are pricking the conscience of the church on that and similar issues. Busters are calling the church back to some of its traditional values, such as respect for family. But churches will need to become more flexible as this diverse group enters into leadership.

Busters are just beginning to financially support their churches. It will be some time before they reach their peak earning years.

Emotionally they will be drawn to give financially to issues and causes close to home. Like the Boomers they also will be inclined to give to projects that prove their worth by ministering effectively to people.

Friendship evangelism will work with Busters, but it will be the twelve-step programs and support-group evangelism events that lead the way. As the most hurting generation to come our way in some time, Busters have many internal needs that will have to be met. Churches that wish to reach unchurched Busters must invest money, leadership, and personal commitment to support-group projects. Churches effectively reaching Busters will focus much of their ministry in their own community rather than around the globe.

The Bridger Wave

Bridgers will eventually point churches toward deeper community. As a generation, they see the church as a place to interact with their friends and family. Bridgers will drive churches toward creative use of technology and raise some significant questions concerning postmodernism along the way.

Bridgers will not be large givers to our churches for many years. Some are just getting started in their jobs and most are still in school. They are likely to support churches that build an authentic sense of community in which they can participate.

Churches that make creative use of opportunities to link and connect with Bridgers stand the best chance of winning them to Christ. Storytelling, apologetics, and interactive learning will be the best ways to evangelize this young generation.

Prepare to Run Some Waves

Running the waves of generational change means we must restructure our ministries so they fit the newer generations. Starting new ministries, restructuring older ones, and eliminating previously successful programs that are no longer effective are difficult steps to take in any situation but can be a major wave to jump in a multigenerational church. The following steps are a composite of ideas suggested by those who have run the generational waves before us.

1. *Bless the past.* When I left my former church to enter the field of church consulting, the church called Dr. Don Weaver to be the pastor. Due to the fact that I was traveling quite a bit and that we had deep roots in the church, Don asked my family to keep attending the church, which we did. On the occasional Sundays that I was there, I was often amazed to hear Pastor Don affirm my ministry publicly before the congregation. He did not do this just to impress me, because people told me he did it when I was not there. I noticed that whenever he publicly affirmed my wife and me, the audience would nod their heads in agreement. And the more he affirmed us, the more the people loved and trusted him.

Unless you are a church planter, you will be building on the foundation of others. It was their commitment, sacrifice, and love for the Lord that brought your church to where it is today. Always pay respect and honor to the past generations and leaders who have served faithfully over the years. If you do so, the congregation will grow in its love for you and your ministry.

2. *Affirm the validity of previous methods and programs.* Over the years priorities and needs change. Some old ministries lose their effectiveness while new ones are born. As an example, take vacation Bible school. In the 1950s VBS was a very effective way to reach children during the summer months. Almost every church had some form of this ministry. But, as far as I am aware, almost no churches had a divorce-recovery group in the 1950s. Today it is almost the reverse. The numerous activities available for children in the twenty-first century have lowered the effectiveness of VBS in some locales, and many churches have stopped using it. But churches add divorce-care groups every day.

Learn what ministries are legendary in the history of your church and begin to affirm them and the people who served in them. It is particularly important to do this with ministries that you are planning to restructure or replace. Let your people know that you understand the place the ministry holds in your church and in their hearts.

3. *Highlight the biblical principles that underlie the previous methods.* Methods and programs are not long-term but the foundational principles that created and supported them are. As you affirm the past leaders and ministries, highlight the foundational principles that undergirded them. For example, a foundational principle that undergirded VBS was evangelism. So, as you affirm VBS, highlight the church's commitment to evangelism. Think through each ministry that will need to be changed and identify the biblical principles that made it valid. Teach and preach the Scripture, the values, and basic principles that are timeless and remain valid today.

4. *Present your new approach as an extension of the past.* Building on the first three steps just noted, present your new approach to ministry as an extension of the former ministry. For example, if your desire is to begin a blended worship service, do not present it as a replacement for a poor worship service that is not meeting needs. Instead, focus on the fact that you are just expanding your existing service so that it will reach more people.

5. *Illustrate how the new approach carries on the values of the former ministry.* One church I worked with wanted to move away from a midweek prayer meeting and Bible study and institute a small-group ministry, with groups meeting several nights a week. In the process of obtaining the congregation's ownership in the new small-group ministry, the pastor and church leaders spent a great deal of time helping the people see that the purpose (value) of the midweek meeting was prayer. They highlighted how the early founders of the church believed that prayer was the main foundation for church effectiveness and that they were correct. Gradually the church leaders demonstrated to the congregation that the new small-group ministry was just building on the founders' commitments and that, in fact, more people would be praying if there were several small groups meeting at different times during the week. The congregation agreed to give it a try, and within one month attendance at the small groups tripled that of the one midweek service.

6. *Assure people that you will be carrying on the tried and true biblical principles of old.* Take time to educate people so that they understand it is the form of the ministry that is changing but not the foundation. Stress the principles of 1 Corinthians 9:19–23 and show how your new ministry is becoming all things to all men so that you might win some. Keep stressing the biblical principles of the past more than the styles of the past, bridging into an explanation of how the newer styles carry on the old principles.

7. *Listen and love.* If the change is major—changing to multiple worship services or becoming blended—take a minimum of one year to work through the above steps. Leaders of multigenerational churches need to give people time to share their feelings, vent their frustrations, and become accustomed to the new ways of ministry. It is wise to provide small forums where a few people can ask questions rather than have a full congregational meeting. Be willing to meet with some people individually as needed to hear their concerns. Much of the time they just want to be assured that they will not be forgotten.

8. *Communicate that traditions are honored best when they are carried on in new ministries.* There are dead traditions and living traditions. Communion is a living tradition because it points us to the past and the future. It causes us to remember the Lord's sacrifice on our behalf and, at the same time, calls us to look for his coming in hope.

Dead traditions continue to be remembered but have little impact on life and people today. But living traditions continue on by providing the historical reason for current ministries. The best traditions are the ones that point to the future through effective ministries that reach people now.

9. *Be patient.* Understand that in urban and suburban areas of the United States, it normally takes five to seven years to turn an existing church in a new direction. In more rural settings it often takes ten to twelve years and sometimes longer. Church leaders who are going through a time of generational change should be careful to take the long view. While we may not be able to accomplish as much this year as we might hope, we will accomplish more over the next five years than we may think.

10. *Trust God to make a way for it all to happen.* The old hymn says it well, "O God, our help in ages past, our hope for years to come." What better words to bear in mind while leading a multi-generational church. As we love God and his people, he will help us lead them to effectively minister to all four generations.

Value Each Other

Whatever the issues, a major role for wave runners is to encourage mutual respect between generations. Throughout the Book of Proverbs younger generations are told to listen to the counsel of the older generation. Older generations, though, should focus on the inherent values of Scripture rather than on the personal habits or stylistic differences the younger generations adopt. Scriptural values, such as honesty, overcoming temptations, wise use of the tongue, and putting God first, are values all generations need to adopt.

There is not much written in Scripture regarding the older generation's respect for the younger. However, some insights might be gained from a study of such passages as, "Fathers, do not exasperate your children, that they may not lose heart" (Col. 3:21); and "Fathers, do not provoke your children to anger; but bring them up in the discipline and instruction of the Lord" (Eph. 6:4). From a generational perspective, the older generation must be careful not to exasperate or provoke the younger generations. Otherwise they may "lose heart" for the church and for Christ.

When Dr. Larry Regenfuss was pastoring South Tacoma Baptist Church in Tacoma, Washington, he recommended the following seven-step plan for cross-generational cooperation, as outlined in Romans 12:10–18.

Step one: Be devoted to one another in love.
Step two: Give preference to one another in honor.
Step three: Be of the same mind toward one another.
Step four: Do not be haughty in mind.

Step five: Do not be wise in your own estimation.

Step six: Respect what is right in the sight of all people.

Step seven: Be at peace with all people.[3]

Conclusion

F. W. Woolworth Company, one of the last great American five-and-dime retail stores, is gone. As a pioneer of the new marketing concept of see-and touch merchandising in 1879, the store was amazingly successful, so much so that in 1913 its founder, Frank Woolworth, built a skyscraper in New York City as his headquarters and paid for it in cash.

Eventually there were Woolworth stores everywhere, but in 1993 almost half of the remaining eight hundred stores closed. Today the Woolworth stores are out of business. Woolworth's problems were partly due to a struggling economy. Its major problem, however, is that it was not able to let go of the past.

Frank Woolworth, who died in 1919, looked to the future and allowed his five-and-dime to change with the times. In 1912 he merged his smaller single stores into a major chain, which positioned him as a giant for years to come. The sad thing is the generations that have followed him in leadership at Woolworth were not able to ride the changes as well as he did.[4]

Running waves on water skis, a Jet Ski, or a Sea-doo is not as easy as it looks. When riders first take to the waves, they usually end up in the water quite a number of times before they get the hang of it. As generational wave runners, we may occasionally find ourselves in the water, and it may be hot rather than cold. But once we get the hang of it, we will find that it is challenging and exciting. Come on now, get on your skis and start running some waves.

Notes

Waves of Change

1. Various authors identify four generations either by dividing the Builders into two cohorts or by adding Boomer grandchildren as an additional generation. For purposes of simplicity, I will look at the Builders as one large generation with the fourth generation being the grandchildren of the Boomers. Readers who are seriously interested in an in-depth analysis of various generations should read the massive book *Generations: The History of America's Future 1584 to 2069* by William Strauss and Neil Howe (New York: Quill, 1991).

2. Bill Nichols, "Democrats See Team as a 'Contrast'" *USA Today* (July 10–12, 1992).

3. For two studies on church size, see Carl F. George, *How to Break Growth Barriers* (Grand Rapids: Baker, 1993) and George Barna, *Today's Pastors* (Ventura, Calif.: Regal, 1993).

4. Carla Wheeler, "Megachurches," *San Bernardino Sun*, July 18, 1993, E.

5. Quoted in Communication Briefings, vol. 4, no. 2 (n.d.). For further information, write Fund-Raising Institute Monthly Portfolio, Box 365, Ambler, PA 19002.

Chapter 1 *What Shaped the Builders?*

1. Douglas Alan Walrath, *Frameworks: Patterns of Living and Believing Today* (New York: Pilgrim Press, 1987).

2. Technically, groups of people who share common frames of reference are called cohorts. A cohort is composed of those who share experiences that uniquely and fundamentally shape them. A cohort may or may not be a complete generation. Indeed there may be several different cohorts within a generational group. Since for the purposes of this book I am speaking in broad terms, I will not deal with individual cohorts.

3. Trent Christman, quoted by Grant Dillman, "Military Broadcasters Are Four Wars Old," *Senior Highlights* (March 1993), 5.

4. Win Arn and Charles Arn, *Live Long and Love It* (Wheaton: Tyndale, 1991), 6. 5. Jeanette Steele, "Staying Power," *Press-Enterprise*, Feb. 15, 1998, H-1.

3. Statistics reported in *L.I.F.E. LINE*, newsletter of the International L.I.F.E. Organization, #17 (n.d.), 3.

Chapter 2 *Builders and the Church*

1. Edmund Fuller, ed., *2,500 Anecdotes for All Occasions* (New York: Avenel, 1970), 119.

2. Thom S. Rainer, *The Bridger Generation* (Nashville: Broadman and Holman, 1997), 169.

3. Donald E. Anderson, "Retire or Refire? Goals for the Final Lap from Philippians" D. Min. diss., Talbot School of Theology, 1990, 24–25.

4. Frank Minirth, John Reed, and Paul Meier, *Beating the Clock: A Guide to Maturing Successfully* (Grand Rapids: Baker, 1985), 13.

5. J. William Mason and Lillian Mason, *You Can Be Happy though Retired* (Dallas: Crescendo, 1979), 107.

6. Auren Uris, *Over 50: The Definitive Guide to Retirement* (Radnor, Penn.: Chilton, 1979), 11.

7. Susan Duerkson, "Growing Older—The Good News and the Bad," *San Diego Union Tribune*, March 26, 2000, B-3.

8. Anderson, *Retire or Refire?* 14–15.

9. Reported by Dr. Mark D. Hayward, associate professor of sociology at Penn State and director of the Gerontology Center.

10. Paul Faulkner, *Making Things Right When Things Go Wrong: Ten Proven Ways to Put Your Life in Order* (Fort Worth: Sweet, 1986), 83.

Chapter 3 *Aging Builders*

1. Lisa Ramirez. "More People Living to Be 100," *San Diego Union Tribune*, Sept. 4, 1999, A-25.

2. Win Arn, "The Church's Challenge and Opportunity of an Aging America . . . ," *The Win Arn Growth Report*, no. 26 (1989).

3. Reported in "Malnutrition among Elders Called Alarming by Experts," in the Riverside/San Bernardino edition of *Senior World*, Jan. 1993, 26.

4. Quoted in "The Center for Aging Resources—Reaching Out to a Graying Population," *Fuller Focus* (fall 1992), 6. For information call the Center for Aging Resources at 818-577-8480.

5. Ibid., 5.

6. "Family Ties Mean More in Times of Crisis, Study Says," Riverside/San Bernardino edition of *Senior World*, Jan. 1993, 27.

7. "Family Caregiving," *The Many Faces of Aging*, fact sheet of the Administration on Aging, May 2001, on the Internet at www.aoa.dhhs.gov/may2001/factsheets/family -caregiving.html.

8. "Widows Adjust to Being Alone," Riverside/San Bernardino edition of *Senior World*, September 1992, 29.

9. See the author's book *Finding Them, Keeping Them* (Nashville: Broadman and Holman Press, 1992) for ideas on how to develop "presence ministries" in a church.

Chapter 4 *Who Are the Boomers?*

1. Death is the natural process that causes generations to decrease in size. Among the relatively youthful and healthy Boomer generation, the deaths that have occurred have been offset by immigrants of the same age group. However, it is predicted by the

Census Bureau that Boomer population will slowly decline to 69 million in 2020, 57 million in 2030, and 37.1 million by 2040. (Shannon Dortch, "Rise and Fall of Generations," *American Demographics* [July 1996], 7.)

2. Walrath, *Frameworks.*

3. For a detailed explanation of the differences between the early and later Boomer cohorts, the reader should see Cheryl Russell, *100 Predictions for the Baby Boom: The Next 50 Years* (New York: Plenum Press, 1987), 41–46.

4. Alice Kahn, "Hey, Hey, They're the Boomers," *San Francisco Chronicle*, March 18, 1992, C1.

5. Quoted by Janet Cawley, "Baby Boomers Ready to Accept Torch," *Chicago Tribune*, Sept. 20, 1992, city edition, 18.

6. Russell, *100 Predictions for the Baby Boom*, 32–33.

7. Irving Kristol, *Reflections of a NeoConservative* (New York: Basic Books, 1983), 27.

8. "Here Come the Baby-Boomers," *U.S. News & World Report* (Nov. 5, 1984), 68.

9. Russell, *100 Predictions for the Baby Boom*, 40.

10. Janet Cawley, quoting Paul Light of the Hubert H. Humphrey Institute at the University of Minnesota, in "Baby Boomers Ready to Accept Torch," 19.

11. Susan Mitchell, "Rock and Roll Will Never Die," *The Boomer Report* 5, no. 6 (June 15, 1993), 7.

12. Phil Goodman, "Radio Still Reaches the Boomers," *The Boomer Report* 5, no. 6 (June 15, 1993), 7.

Chapter 5 *Boomer Believers*

1. Elmer L. Towns, "Reaching the Baby Boomer," *Church Growth Today* 5, no. 5 (1990), 1.

2. Lyle E. Schaller, "Whatever Happened to the Baby Boomers?" *Newsletter* (1985), 9.

3. Wade Clark Roof, *A Generation of Seekers: The Spiritual Journeys of the Baby Boom Generation* (San Francisco: HarperCollins, 1993).

4. Peter Steinfels, "Charting the Currents of Belief for the Generation That Rebelled," *New York Times*, May 30, 1993.

5. Reported in "The Church Around the World," *Tyndale House Newsletter* (October 1992), 2.

6. Quoted by Steinfels, "Charting the Currents."

7. Leith C. Anderson, "A Senior Pastor's Perspective on Baby Boomers," *Christian Education Journal* 11, no. 1 (autumn 1990), 75.

8. James Scudder, "Renewed Search for Faith," *San Bernardino Sun*, Feb. 10, 1990, D4.

9. Ibid.

10. For further insight on the case of Boomers returning to the church, see George Barna, "The Case of the Mission Boomers," *Ministry Currents* 2, no. 1 (Jan.–March, 1992), 1–4.

11. Kenneth Briggs, "Baby Boomers: Boom or Bust for the Churches?" *Progressions*, A Lilly Endowment Occasional Report 2, no. 1 (Jan. 1990), 7.

12. Quoted in "Successfully Reaching Baby Boomers," *Mandate: A Home Missions Magazine for the Wesleyan Church* (Indianapolis: The Wesleyan Church), 15.

13. James F. Engel, "We Are the World," *Christianity Today* (Sept. 24, 1990), 33.

14. Mike Bellah, *Baby Boom Believers* (Wheaton: Tyndale House, 1988), 129.

Chapter 6 *Reaching the Boomer Generation*

1. Walter Hatch, "Election Analysts See 'Baby Boom' Voters' Influence," *Seattle Times,* Nov. 12, 1989.

2. Quoted by Jeannye Thornton, "Those City Lights," *U.S. News & World Report* (March 4, 1985), 61.

3. For complete details see Roof, *A Generation of Seekers.*

4. Don Lattin, "Fast-Track Baby Boomers Slow for God," *San Bernardino Sun,* Nov. 25, 1989, religion section.

5. Quoted in "Staying on the Marriage Track in the 1990s," *USA Today* (March 1990), 10.

6. Quoted by Walter Shapiro, "The Birth and—Maybe—Death of Yuppiedom," *Time* (April 8, 1991), 65.

7. Quoted by Joan Smith, "Let Us Pray," *San Francisco Examiner,* June 6, 1993, D5.

8. Margaret L. Udansky, "Baby Boomers Hit Brakes after Life in the Fast Lane," *USA Today,* June 24, 1993, A10.

9. Melvyn Kinder, *Going Nowhere Fast* (New Jersey: Prentice Hall, 1990).

10. Reported by John Case, "The Real Age Wave," *INC* (July 1989), 23.

11. Quoted by Steinfels, "Charting the Currents of Belief for the Generation That Rebelled."

12. Stepfamily Association of America, "Stepfamily Fact Sheet" (June 10, 2000), 2.

13. Quoted in "Successfully Reaching Baby Boomers," 15.

14. "Where Singles Are Most Numerous," *U.S. News & World Report* (May 13, 1996).

15. Elmer Towns, "How to Reach the Baby Boomer," a seminar presented by the Church Growth Institute, P.O. Box 4404, Lynchburg, VA 24502 (Jan. 1990).

Chapter 7 *Why Are They Called Busters?*

1. "Simpsons Help Save a Life," *San Bernardino Sun,* May 25, 1992, D6.

2. Bill Marvel and Melissa Morrison, "The Pacifier People," *Dallas Morning News,* February 7, 1993, F1.

3. George Shultz, quoted by Richard Saul Wurman in *Information Anxiety* (New York: Doubleday, 1989), 41, 309.

4. Marvel and Morrison, "The Pacifier People," F1.

5. Ibid., F4.

6. Louise Palmer, "Abortion Losing Its Appeal to Women of GenX," *San Diego Union Tribune,* Sept. 5, 1999, G-1.

7. David M. Gross and Sophfronia Scott, "Proceeding with Caution," *Time* (July 16, 1990), 58.

8. Pamela Paul, "The EchoBoomerang," *American Demographics* (June 2001), 46.

9. Alan Deutschman, "What 25-Year-Olds Want," *Fortune* (Aug. 27, 1990), 43.

10. Lisa E. Philips, "Love, American Style," *American Demographics* (Feb. 1999), 56.

Chapter 8 *Busters and the Church*

1. Marvel and Morrison, "The Pacifier People," F4.

2. Alice Kahn and Shann Nix, "Who's Stressed and Who's Blessed," *San Francisco Chronicle,* July 12, 1993.

Chapter 9 *Reaching Busters*

1. Paul, "The EchoBoomerang," 52.

2. Clark Morphew, "Bringing 'Buster' Generation to Religion," *Press-Enterprise* (March 6, 1993).

Chapter 10 *When Did the Bridgers Arrive?*

1. Some demographers define the Bridger generation as those born between 1977 and 1994. The reason is that another baby boom occurred during those years. It was similar to that of the Boomer generation when births topped the charts in 1946 at 3,289,000 and grew each year until they peaked in 1964 at 4,027,000. Between 1965 and 1976, annual births dropped from 3,760,000 to 3,168,000. This drop in total births became popularly known as the Baby Bust. But beginning in 1977 births began to rise again from 3,327,000 to a peak of 4,158,000 in 1993. The total number of people born between 1977 and 1994 was roughly 72 million, just shy of the 76 million of the Baby Boom. Clearly the period between 1977 and 1994 was another baby boom. However, in *One Church, Four Generations*, I have chosen to call those born from 1977 to 1983 the Boomlet and group them under the Buster generation.

2. Reported in "ChurchChampionsFax" 4, no. 6 (March 22, 1999).

3. Frank Feather, *future consumer.com* (Toronto: Warwick, 2000), 37.

4. Thomas Middelhoff, "Fast Talk," *Fast Company* (May 2000), 86.

5. Quoted by Katharine Mieszkowski in "How to Speed Up Your Startup," *Fast Company* (May 2000), 141.

6. Quoted by Vivian Marino, "Generation E Is Studying Reading, 'Riting 'n' Retailing," *San Diego Union-Tribune*, Sunday, Aug. 24, 1997.

7. "Phone Home," *American Demographics* (Dec. 2001), 18.

8. Quoted in "Just Surfin' Through," *American Demographics* (Jan. 2000), 12. Contact Forrester Research at 617-497-7090.

9. Quoted by Helene Stapinski, "Ynot Love?" *American Demographics* (Feb. 1999), 63.

10. Quoted by Lisa Bannon, "Little Big Spenders," *Wall Street Journal*, Oct. 13, 1998, 1.

11. Anthony Perkins, "The Angler," *Red Herring* (Nov. 2001), 16.

Chapter 11 *Bridgers and the Church*

1. Adapted from "Feeling Old," Beloit College, Wisconsin, January 2000.

2. Quoted in "Books to Come . . . What People Will Be Reading in the Future," Net-Fax, Sept. 28, 1998.

3. Susan Mitchell, "The Next Baby Boom," *American Demographics* (Oct. 1995), 25.

Chapter 12 *Winning Bridgers*

1. Ron Hutchcraft, "Reaching the Global Youth Culture," 2001, http://www.gospelcom.net/lpea/firstpriority/spring2001/pf_feature_hutchcraft.shtml.

Chapter 13 *Reading the Waves*

1. Quoted by Julian Marias in *Generations: A Historical Method* (Alabama: University of Alabama Press, 1967), 4.

2. Susan Mitchell, *Generation X: Americans Aged 18 to 34* (New York: New Strategist, 2001).

3. *The Millennials: Americans under Age 25* (New York: New Strategist, 2001).

4. Howard Reich, "Will the Symphony Orchestra Survive?" *San Diego Union Tribune,* Nov. 18, 2001, F-8.

Chapter 14 *Linking Generations*

1. "2,024 sq. ft. Showcase Home Built by Consumer Research," *San Bernardino Sun,* May 26, 1993, A7.

2. John C. LaRue, Jr. "Worship Style Synthesis," *Your Church* (Nov./Dec. 2001), 72.

3. Portions of this section originally appeared in the *McIntosh Church Growth Network Newsletter* 1, no. 7 (1989).

Chapter 15 *Wave Runners*

1. Eric Sevareid, "A New Stage," *Modern Maturity* (April–May 1991), 73.

2. Douglas Murren, "Reaching Boomers," *Ministries Today* (Jan.–Feb. 1989).

3. Adapted from Larry Regenfuss, "What Do You Mean, 'Common Sense'?" an unpublished research paper (Jan. 1990), 41–42.

4. Adapted from Arnold Garson, "Woolworth Should Have Changed with Times," *San Bernardino Sun,* Oct. 17, 1993, D.

Resources

General

Anderson, Leith. *Dying for Change*. Minneapolis: Bethany House, 1990.

Austin, Joe, and Michael Nevin Willard, eds. *Generations of Youth: Youth Cultures and History in Twentieth-Century America*. New York: New York University Press, 1998.

Bloom, Allan. *The Closing of the American Mind*. New York: Simon and Schuster, 1987.

Chandler, Russell. *Racing toward 2001*. Grand Rapids: Zondervan, 1992.

Dychtwald, Ken. *Age Wave*. Los Angeles: Jeremy P. Tarcher, 1989.

Gerber, Jerry, et al. *Life-Trends: Your Future for the Next 30 Years*. New York: Avon Books, 1991.

Hine, Thomas. "The Rise and Decline of the Teenager," *American Heritage*. Sept. 1999, 70–82.

Lasch, Christopher. *The Culture of Narcissism*. New York: Warner Communications, 1979.

Mannheim, Karl. "The Problem of Generations," chapter 7 in *Essays on the Sociology of Knowledge*. London: Routledge and Kesan Paul, 1952.

Marias, Julian. *Generations: A Historical Method*. Alabama: University of Alabama Press, 1967.

McIntosh, Gary L., and Glen S. Martin. *The Issachar Factor: Understanding the Trends Confronting Your Church and Designing a Strategy for Success*. Nashville: Broadman and Holman, 1994.

Postman, Neil. *Amusing Ourselves to Death*. New York: Elisabeth Sifton Books, 1985.

Scifres, Mary J. *Searching for Seekers: Ministry with a New Generation of the Unchurched*. Nashville: Abingdon Press, 1998.

Smith, J. Walker, and Ann Clurman. *Rocking the Ages*. New York: HarperCollins, 1997.

Strauss, William, and Neil Howe. *The Fourth Turning*. New York: Broadway Books, 1997.

————. *Generations: The History of America's Future 1584 to 2069*. New York: Quill, 1991.

Toffler, Alvin. *Previews and Premises*. New York: Random House, 1983.

Walrath, Douglas Alan. *Frameworks: Patterns of Living and Believing Today*. New York: Pilgrim Press, 1987.

Wattenberg, Ben J. *The Birth Dearth*. New York: Pharos Books, 1987.

Whitesel, Bob, and Kent R. Hunter. *A House Divided: Bridging the Generation Gaps in Your Church*. Nashville: Abingdon Press, 2000.

The Builder Wave

Alive: A Magazine for Christian Senior Adults, P.O. Box 46464, Cincinnati, OH 45246-0464, 513-825-3681.

Anderson, Don. *Keep the Fire!* Sisters, Ore.: Multnomah Books, 1994.

Arn, Win, and Charles Arn. *Live Long and Love It!* Wheaton: Tyndale House, 1991.

Brokaw, Tom. *The Greatest Generation*. New York: Random House, 1998.

Fifty-Plus Contact, a magazine for adults over 50, 2450 Milltower Ct., Mississauga, Ontario L5N 5Z6, 905-542-7400 x 5261.

Jakes, P. David. *The Decision Is Yours*. Nashville: LifeWay Press, 1995.

L.I.F.E. LINE, the newsletter of the International L.I.F.E. Organization, 1857 Highland Oaks, Arcadia, CA 91006, 818-355-2470.

Mason, J. William, and Lillian Mason. *You Can Be Happy though Retired*. Dallas: Crescendo, 1979.

Minirth, Frank, John Reed, and Paul Meier. *Beating the Clock: A Guide to Maturing Successfully*. Grand Rapids: Baker, 1985.

Modern Maturity Magazine, 3200 E. Carson St., Lakewood, CA 90712.

Thau, Richard D., and Jay S. Heflin, eds. *Generations Apart: Xers vs. Boomers vs. the Elderly*. New York: Prometheus Books, 1997.

Uris, Auren. *Over 50: The Definitive Guide to Retirement*. Radnor, Penn.: Chilton, 1979.

The Boomer Wave

Bast, Robert L. *The Missing Generation*. Monrovia, Calif.: Church Growth, 1991.

Bellah, Mike. *Baby Boom Believers*. Wheaton: Tyndale House, 1988.

The Boomer Report, 641 Avenue of the Americas, 4th Floor, New York, NY 10011, 800-298-5699.

Boutilier, Robert. *Targeting Families: Marketing to and through the New Family*. Ithaca, N.Y.: American Demographics, 1993.

Collins, Gary R., and Timothy E. Clinton. *Baby Boomer Blues*. Dallas: Word, 1992.

Cork, David. *The Pig and the Python: How to Prosper from the Aging Baby Boom*. Toronto: Prima Publishing, 1998.

Engel, James F., and Jerry D. Jones. *Baby Boomers and the Future of World Missions.* Orange, Calif.: Management Development, 1989.

Frinzel, Hans. *Help! I'm a Baby Boomer.* Wheaton: Victor Books, 1989.

Hamilton, Neil A. et al. *Atlas of the Baby Boom Generation.* New York: Macmillan Library Reference, 2000.

Jones, Landen Y. *Great Expectations.* New York: Coward, McCann, and Geophegan, 1980.

Light, Paul C. *Baby Boomers.* New York: W. W. Norton, 1988.

Murren, Doug. *The Baby Boomerang.* Ventura, Calif.: Regal Books, 1990.

Nichols, Michael P. *Turning Forty in the Eighties: Personal Crisis, Time for Change.* New York: W. W. Norton, 1986.

"Reaching Generation X," entire issue of *Strategies for Today's Leaders.* Jan.–March 1998, vol. 35, no. 1.

Roof, Wade Clark. *A Generation of Seekers: The Spiritual Journeys of the Baby Boom Generation.* San Francisco: HarperCollins, 1993.

———. *Spiritual Marketplace: Baby Boomers and the Remaking of American Religion.* New Jersey: Princeton University Press, 1999.

Russell, Cheryl. *100 Predictions for the Baby Boom: The Next 50 Years.* New York: Plenum Press, 1987.

———. *The Master Trend: How the Baby Boom Generation Is Reshaping America.* New York: Plenum Press, 1993.

Wallechivsky, David. *Midterm Report: The Class of 1965.* New York: Viking Penguin Press, 1986.

Walrath, Douglas Alan. *Frameworks: Patterns of Living and Believing Today.* New York: Pilgrim Press, 1987.

Wolfe, David B. *Marketing to Boomers and Beyond.* New York: McGraw-Hill, 1993.

The Buster Wave

Barna, George. *Generation Next.* Ventura: Regal Books, 1995.

———. *The Invisible Generation: Baby Busters.* Glendale, Calif.: Barna Research Group, 1992.

Beaudin, Tom. *Virtual Faith: The Irreverent Spiritual Quest of Generation X.* San Francisco: Jossey-Bass, 1998.

Bradford, Lawrence, and Claire Raines. *Twentysomething.* New York: MasterMedia Limited, 1992.

Celek, Tim, and Dieter Zander. *Inside the Soul of a New Generation.* Grand Rapids: Zondervan, 1996.

Coupland, Doug. *Generation X: Tales for an Accelerated Culture.* New York: St. Martin's Press, 1991.

Dunn, William. *The Baby Bust: A Generation Comes of Age.* Ithaca, N.Y.: American Demographics, 1993.

Flory, Richard W., and Donald E. Miller, eds. *GenX Religion.* New York: Routledge, 2000.

Ford, Kevin Graham. *Jesus for a New Generation.* Downers Grove, Ill.: InterVarsity Press, 1995.

Gerber, Jerry, et al. *Life-Trends: Your Future for the Next 30 Years.* New York: Avon Books, 1989.

Gibb, Steven. *Twentysomething, Floundering, and Off the Yuppie Track.* Chicago: The Noble Press, 1992.

Hahn, Todd, and David Verhaagen. *GenXers after God: Helping a Generation Pursue Jesus.* Grand Rapids: Baker, 1998.

———. *Reckless Hope: Understanding and Reaching Baby Busters.* Grand Rapids: Baker, 1996.

Howe, Neil, and Bill Strauss. *13th GEN: Abort, Retry, Ignore, Fail?* New York: Vintage, 1993.

Ianni, Francis. *The Search for Structure: A Report on American Youth Today.* New York: The Free Press, 1989.

Koons, Carolyn A., and Michael J. Anthony. *Single Adult Passages.* Grand Rapids: Baker, 1991.

Littwin, Susan. *The Postponed Generation.* New York: Quill, 1987.

Loeb, Paul Rogat. *Generation at the Crossroads.* New Brunswick, N.J.: Rutgers University Press, 1994.

Long, Jimmy. *Generating Hope: A Strategy for Reaching the Postmodern Generation.* Downers Grove: InterVarsity Press, 1997.

Mahedy, William, and Janet Bernardi. *A Generation Alone.* Downers Grove, Ill.: InterVarsity Press, 1994.

Sacks, Peter. *Generation X Goes to College.* Chicago: Carus Publishing, 1996.

Sciacca, Fran. *Generation at Risk.* Chicago: Moody Press, 1990.

The Bridger Wave

"Is This Generation Lost?" *WCA News,* entire Sept.–Oct. 2001 issue, magazine of the Willow Creek Association.

Rainer, Thom S. *The Bridger Generation.* Nashville: Broadman and Holman, 1997.

Schneider, Barbara, and David Stevenson. *The Ambitious Generation: America's Teenagers, Motivated but Directionless.* New Haven: Yale University Press, 1999.

Zoba, Wendy. "The Class of '00," *Christianity Today,* Feb. 3, 1997, 18–28.

———. *Generation 2K: What Parents and Others Need to Know About the Millennials.* Downers Grove, Ill.: InterVarsity Press, 1999.

Organizations

AARP (American Association of Retired Persons), 1909 K St. NW, Washington, DC 20049, 202-872-4700, www.aarp.org.

AARP Grandparents Information Center, Dept. C, 601 E Street NW, Washington, D.C. 20049, www.gic@aarp.org.

AFL-CIO Dept. of Community Services, 815 16th St. NW, Washington, DC 20006, 202-637-5189.

The Alzheimer's Association, 800-621-0379.

American Council of Life Insurance, 1001 Pennsylvania Ave. NW, Washington, DC 20004, 202-624-2000.

American Physical Therapy Association, 1111 North Fairfax St., Alexandria, VA 22314-1488, 800-999-2782.

Area Agency on Aging, refer to the white pages of your local phone directory.

The Brookdale Center on Aging, 425 E. 25th St., New York, NY 10010-2590, 212- 481-7670, for locating a "respite-care" program in your area.

Christian Association of Prime Timers (CAP), 800-443-0227, an organization offering assistance to Builders.

Christian Association of Senior Adult Ministries (CASA), 27601 Forbes Rd., #49, Laguna Niquel, CA 92677, 888-200-8552, fax 949-582-1396, info@gocasa.org, www.gocasa.org.

Christian Seniors Fellowship, P.O. Box 46464, Cincinnati, OH 45246-0464, 513-825-3681. A nonprofit corporation organized for and by Christian senior adults; provides resource ideas for ministering to Builders.

Forever Young, First Evangelical Free Church, 2801 North Brea Blvd., Fullerton, CA 92835, 714-529-5544.

Foundation for Hospice and Home Care, 519 C St. NE, Washington, DC 20002, 202-547-6586.

Gray Panthers, 1424 16th St., Suite 602, Washington, DC 20036.

L.I.F.E. International, 1857 Highland Oaks Dr., Arcadia, CA 91006, 818-355-2470, provides seminars and consulting to help churches start ministries to senior adults.

The National Alliance for the Mentally Ill, 800-950-6264.

National Association of Baby Boomers, 1722 Ohearn Lane, DePere, WI 54115, 920-983-6482.

National Council of Senior Citizens, 925 15th St. NW, Washington, DC 20005, 202-347-8800.

National Council on the Aging, 600 Maryland Ave. SW, Washington, DC 20024, 202-479-1200.

National Home Caring Council, 519 C St. NE, Washington, DC 20002, 202-547-6586.

National Institute on Aging, Federal Building, Room 6C12, Bethesda, MD 20892, 301-496-1752.

National Institute on Drug Abuse, Elder Education, P.O. Box 416, Kensington, MD 20740.

Rolling Hills Covenant Church, 2222 Palos Verdes Dr. North, Rolling Hills Est., CA 90274, 310-519-9406.

Stepfamily Association of America, 650 J Street, Suite 205, Lincoln NE 68508, 800-735-0329, www.saafamilies.org.

Web Sites

American Fact Finder, http://factfinder.census.gov.

www.baylor.edu/~Scott_Moore/Xnty_Pmism.html—a site on Christian faith and post-modernity.

www.churchdoctor.com—church consulting firm offering insights on multigenerations.

www.focus.org.uk—a site focusing on resources to engage postmodern culture.

www.marshillforum.org—the site of the Mars Hill forum, a Christian nonprofit organization that seeks to reveal Christ to the post-Christian culture.

www.strategiesfortoday.org—helpful resource for reaching all generations.

www.mcintoshcgn.com—a site offering articles and resources on biblical church growth.

www.millennials.com—a site offering the latest articles and insights on Generation X and Generation Y.

www.next-wave.org—a site discussing the nature of ministry in the twenty-first century.

www.onmission.com—a site with resources related to sharing Christ in the real world.

www.regenerator.com—the site of *Regeneration Quarterly,* targeted at postmoderns.

www.theyoungsenior.com—on-line magazine for adults over 50.

www.youngleader.org/coolstuff.html—a reference for an extensive list of books regarding the emergence of young leaders under forty years of age.

The McIntosh
Church Growth
Network

D r. Gary L. McIntosh is a nationally known author, speaker, consultant, and professor of Christian Ministry and Leadership at Talbot School of Theology, Biola University, located in La Mirada, California. He has written extensively in the fields of pastoral ministry, leadership, generational studies, and church growth.

Dr. McIntosh is a graduate of Colorado Christian University, Western Conservative Baptist Seminary, and Fuller Theological Seminary. He holds degrees in biblical studies, pastoral studies, and church growth studies.

As president of the McIntosh Church Growth Network, a church-consulting firm he founded in 1989, Dr. McIntosh has served more than five hundred churches in fifty-three denominations throughout the United States and Canada. He is the recipient of the Distinguished Faculty Award from Biola Universty, the Distinguished Alumni Award from Colorado Christian University, and the Donald McGavran Award in church growth from the American Society for Church Growth.

Dr. McIntosh speaks to numerous churches, organizations, schools, and conventions each year. Ministry services available include keynote presentations at major meetings, seminars and workshops, training courses, and ongoing consultation.

To arrange for a live presentation of the material found in *One Church, Four Generations* or to request a catalog of materials or other information on Dr. McIntosh's availability and ministry, contact:

The McIntosh Church Growth Network
P.O. Box 892589
Temecula, CA 92589-2589
909-506-3086
E-mail: cgnet@mac.com
Internet: www.mcintoshcgn.com

Beyond the First Visit